Praise for 7

"If you're struggling with challenge, adversity, or overwhelm, *Tsunami to Greatness* will bring you hope and show you what's possible. Maria Mantoudakis's remarkable account of the many miracles throughout her life is an inspiration. Through applying the Universal laws and practices offered in this book, you can live your greatest life."

> — Marci Shimoff, #1 *NY Times* bestselling author, *Happy for No Reason* and *Chicken Soup for the Woman's Soul*

"A tsunami of gems await you in Maria Mantoudakis's first book, *Tsunami to Greatness*. With candor, clarity, and compassion Maria helps us see our our struggles in life with new eyes and discover the gifts they bring. This book is like having your very own up-close-and-personal guide for being an artist of life, living true to your Self. Wisdom on every page!"

> — Dr. Kymn Harvin, international best-selling author of *The Soul of America Speaks: Wisdom for Healing and Moving Forward*

"*Tsunami to Greatness* shines a unique perspective on the true self, where our high vibration feelings of peace, love and gratefulness reside. Maria Mantoudakis provides real world insight on how to access our true self and live a fulfilling, joyous and purposeful life."

— Chris Curran, author of *Leap Beyond Your Limits*

"If you are stuck in a rut and feel like you are just going through the motions every day, existing but not really living, *Tsunami to Greatness* will help you identify your purpose and start living a transformed life that makes a difference in this world. Maria Mantoudakis shares her heart and experiences to empower you to achieve your greatness and become the best version of you."

— Wendy Off Gonzalez, Corporate Training
    Consultant

I would like to dedicate this book with never-ending
love to my son, Georgio.
You are my inspiration. Your kindness, love, creativity,
talents, intelligence, and dedication light up the world. You
fill my heart with gratitude for the miracle that you are.

 Published by: Capucia, LLC
211 Pauline Drive #513
York, PA 17402

Paperback ISBN: 978-1-954920-00-2
eBook ISBN: 978-1-954920-01-9
Library of Congress Control Number: 2021902994

Cover Design: Ranilo Cabo
Layout: Ranilo Cabo
Editor and Proofreader: Jennifer Crosswhite
Book Midwife: Carrie Jareed

Printed in the United States of America

Tsunami
to
Greatness

Unleashing the Power of Self-Love
and Synchronicity to Become the
Best Version of You

MARIA MANTOUDAKIS

CONTENTS

Preface

Wherever you are in your life right now, you may be looking at your life with a happy smile, or you may be looking at it as a tough journey. Although right now I look at my life and smile, when I look back there were so many phases in my life that felt like I was punched in the stomach; I couldn't breathe, I couldn't cope, I didn't know how to take the next step. I was living a nightmare, having a total breakdown. It felt like the end of the world. Yet, not only did I survive, I found myself moving in an upward spiral. I became a new person. Every personal tsunami in my life has been a promotion, a transformation, a step forward in my journey to personal greatness. The change is so drastic, that often I look back at the version of me I left behind and feel compassion and love and forgiveness because I did not have the wisdom or knowledge that I do now.

The new me knows what the old me just didn't know. I know that my problems then were so big because I was smaller. The same problems now seem so small because I have grown bigger spiritually than they are. Through the tsunamis in my life I became a greater version of myself. Every single person goes through some kind of a tsunami in their life. Yet when we are going through it, we feel like we are the only ones who have ever experienced anything as traumatic and painful as we are experiencing.

If you are going through a tsunami right now, my love and compassion embrace you. I can tell you with certainty that you will survive. You are not alone; your life will be bright and lovely and full of joy. This is part of the ride; it is part of your personal promotion and you are about to experience a happiness and joy you have not felt before. My wish is that you will allow this book to inspire you while you are going through the tough times and also through the rainbow after the storm. Thank you for reading this book, for allowing me to speak to you, because I truly care. I am hoping that the perspective, as well as the tools and practices, will support your healing process and get you to the other side of that rainbow fast. Tsunamis used to be the end of the world. They are not the end of the world any more. They are just a pause, a storm, to be followed by a step up and a beautiful rainbow…

Life

Life is meant to be filled with joy and wonder. It is meant to be filled with happiness, love, abundance, health. In order for us to reach that level, we are sometimes faced with some contradiction. Most people in the world are far from achieving the life I describe. Everywhere we turn there is pain, struggle, suffering. It is so difficult watching the news these days. A feeling of overwhelm comes upon us, as we wish we could change it all. We know deeply that it is not supposed to be this way, or is it? We know that sometimes there is a huge gap between the way things are supposed to be and the way things are. Although when we view the world it seems overwhelming, fixing it starts with me and you. If each individual found the peace, the love, the joy, the abundance, the health they deserve, if each individual loved themselves and loved everyone around them, the world would be a different place. Everyone seems to expect for someone else to step in and fix the world. It doesn't seem to work that way. The world isn't someone else. It is us. It is you and me.

As I was writing the last chapters of this book, the Coronavirus pandemic was upon us. It seems that all the fear, sadness, worry that was going on in the world about other issues paused as we faced something we never really imagined. A great life lesson is to never worry about the future. Think of the 9/11/2001 events at the World Trade Center, Washington DC, Pennsylvania, and across the United States. Prior to this event we worried about everything else. Never did we imagine these horrific events. The Coronavirus pandemic is another example. Experiencing this in the United States, we went from normal life--going to work, meeting with people, etc.--to immediate social distancing and stay-at-home directives. We worried about so many other things, but never a pandemic.

So why do we worry about things? Worry starts as a fearful thought that keeps growing and becomes a huge giant that overtakes us into total devastation, into a personal tsunami.

As I am writing this, everyone throughout the world is going through this personal tsunami. It is a pandemic that is in our world, with a series of events that everyone wishes were not taking place. It is overwhelming; there seems to be no escape. One cannot say, "I will go to another place where this is not happening," because it is happening everywhere.

Since the beginning of human life, it has been the hope in everyone's heart to have a world filled with love, peace, joy, and happiness. Do we see how this pandemic may create a trajectory that will take us toward these things? The struggle is global, the fear is common, everyone identifies with each other's pain. We realize that every human being wants the same thing: to be well, to be loved, to be cared for, to be at peace, to be abundant, to be healthy. Who is our enemy right now? COVID-19. We forgot our enemies; we are just looking to help each other get through this situation. This pandemic is making us look beyond our differences, beyond enemies, race, religion, country. It is making us into people of compassion who desire the well-being of all other people in the world. I look forward to a world where people remember all that we learned and are still learning through this pandemic. A world where we remember how much love we sent out to all people as we realized that we are all one. A world where we forget what separates us, and we remember what unites us, our human being-ness, our spiritual oneness.

My friend Deborah lives in Brazil. She has noticed the changes in our environment since the start of social distancing and people staying at home. She noticed how there is less pollution now, how there are more animals in the forest during her walks. My cousin Ada in Greece was telling me how on her early morning walks she could feel a renewal in the earth, and at night she can see more stars than ever before. For the last few years, our children have been expressing their concern about global warming, and in their hearts was a world with less pollution, a world where we care for our planet. Now our mother earth can breathe because there are fewer people driving, fewer airplanes flying, and as it is springtime, the grass is growing greener and the flowers are blooming in a cleaner planet. Is this what will bring us to what we always hoped for?

Tsunami—Wisdom, Hope, Faith
A journey back to what we already knew

We all have our life journey. It seems that this is a journey of remembering what we always knew. When we start our life as babies, we seem to understand a lot about life. We are happy, we are filled with love, we anticipate all will be all right and we will be taken care of. We feel abundant; we live in the present. As the years go by, everyone around us can't wait to teach us all we should know. In this process, we learn how to be human. We learn how to live life as most people live it, as a struggle, a competition for survival, for social status, for acceptance. As we live, we gain knowledge, and we learn a lot of lessons. This knowledge and experience becomes our filter through which we see the world and by which we live our life.

At any given moment we can choose to grow or to be at a standstill when we become stuck in the disappointment of the past or the fear of the future. If we choose to grow, our journey becomes an upward spiral. We find ourselves evolving through many versions of ourselves, an evolution of self where we become stronger and more resilient as we grow. If we allow our filters to stop our growth, if we keep replaying our past or are fearful of the future, we find ourselves in a continuous personal tsunami. Life becomes very overwhelming. In this state of despair, we often feel like we have lost it all. It is a state of negativity that continues to grow and becomes a downward spiral. It leaves us in a state of not knowing what to do, feeling like a tsunami has hit us and we are hopelessly trying to stay above water. We lose hope. We find ourselves in total despair. The art of getting out of this state comes from wisdom, hope and faith--the things we often lack when we are in this state.

Wisdom, Hope, Faith

The upward journey starts by knowing there is a way out and having the wisdom to realize that the way we are seeing things may be distorted because we are viewing our life through our own filters. It is a journey of understanding our thoughts and beliefs and being open to healing the pain. It is the struggle of quieting down our inner negative thoughts and minimizing our internal chaos. The wisdom is knowing that there is a positive way out. Even if we are not able to see the final destination, we must know that there is a next step, and whatever we are experiencing is only temporary. When you hit bottom, you are living the worst and most difficult stage. We need to know that there are many stages in our transformation, including stages that bring about peace, ease, happiness, and flow. Each of these stages are part of our journey toward our continual greatness. You need to hold on to that wisdom and have faith that a small shift will help you start your journey upwards.

Hope and faith are what actually get us there. During extreme hardships, hope and faith are the key to getting out of the hardship and on to the other side. Holocaust survivors confirmed that those who survived were the ones who envisioned the day of freedom, the ones who saw beyond their reality in concentration camps. Through their mind's eye they could see themselves living life outside of their then circumstances.

We have a beautiful mind that has the capability to transport us to anywhere we want to be. In times of despair, it is the time to let go of the current situation, the current events, the despair of the news. You must see the sunshine of tomorrow in order to get out of the stormy circumstances of today. My friend Ron always tells me, "I am from Missouri; you must show me." But I am thinking, "Ron, it doesn't work that way. Seeing is not believing. You must believe it in order to see it." You must believe that tomorrow will be different from today, and that the current condition is only as permanent as we choose to make it. Believing that tomorrow will be better will bring tomorrow's better circumstances.

Sometimes I see life like a high-rise building with an unlimited number of floors. The view on the higher floors is different than the view on the first floor. As we move up the floors of our transformation, we can see different views, and as we move upwards, there is less noise, less chaos, more order and beauty. I remember in 1969 watching the astronauts when they first walked on the moon. There was our Planet Earth that looked like a beautiful blue star behind them; beautiful and peaceful. Who could imagine all that was going on in the world, and who can imagine all the different experiences every human being was having at that time? As you keep zooming in closer and closer, you can see the details--the beauty of the earth--but you can also see the devastation of the human experience and the storms that rage.

This is our life journey; its purpose is reaching the highest possible level of Your Greatness. Life is the journey to the very best version of yourself. It is an upward journey. It is a journey toward continuous awakening and transformation. Yes, there is a state of peace, happiness, joy, abundance, health, love. There is a place of wisdom, understanding, unending bliss, a place where you look back at your life and see, just like the astronauts did, a beautiful view.

The book will guide you through its two parts. The first part provides you with step-by-step wisdom. If you are in a life tsunami right now, it will provide the initial steps to get out of the anxiety and stress you are feeling. As you begin seeing the light, it empowers you to take control of your inner voice as well as any fear and negative thinking. You will become aware of your personal filters and will be introduced to your human, as well as true self. As you understand all aspects of yourself, you can feel the thrill of accepting and loving yourself. When we let others into our life, the book gives you tools to deal with the criticism and judgment of others as well as handling our judgments and our ego's need to always be right.

Part two guides us through universal laws and practices. The twelve universal laws that are in play in your life are explained, including the most popular of these laws, the Law of Attraction. Practices in part two include considering our life purpose, gratefulness, forgiveness, and being aware of how to raise our vibrational frequency, as well as provide techniques for releasing. Within part two you will also explore miracles, letting go of worry, expecting things that others may view as impossible as things of great possibility. The Greatness chapter opens the door to understanding that all our experiences, and that everything in life moves us toward our next level of greatness.

Recently, I conducted a market research project asking participants who felt stuck in their life, what was the number one cause of not making a change, of not embracing life transformation. The number one fear that kept people from embracing change is fear of the unknown. So many people prefer living stuck and unhappy, because they are so fearful of making a change that may bring them a more undesirable result than their current state.

In this book I will empower you to let go of that fear. How will I do that? By providing you with a deeper understanding of your belief system, your filters, and your thinking. I will take you on a journey of understanding and loving all aspects of yourself, understanding the Universe, and a glimpse into a life of joy, love, abundance, health, and all that you desire.

Regardless of where you are in your journey, you are welcome to hop onto the upward spiral movement, receive the awareness, and join the transformation to Your Greatness.

Part 1

Chapter 1

Hitting Bottom

Being defeated is often a temporary condition.
Giving up is what makes it permanent.
—Marilyn vos Savant

As I sit at Starbucks, right next to me are young people talking about their lives. When I was a teenager, the conversations were about school, about boys (or girls), about an upcoming party, about our parents. We had fears of getting in trouble with our parents and teachers, getting picked on in school, the boy that we liked not liking us, the friend who was not our friend anymore, getting good grades.

The conversations have changed throughout the years. The stories now have an additional intensity. "I can't do this anymore" is a very common phrase. "Depression," "panic," "suicide" are other popular words. The strange thing is, the listeners rarely react, because these seem to be normal words,

13

normal conversations. Concerns about school shootings and climate change seem to be the current running underneath every day events. Getting picked on has taken a new dimension, now done through social media and getting wider participation.

But it doesn't stop with teenagers. Suicide rates have risen to the upper forty percentiles in the United States. So many people have hit bottom, feeling trapped, losing hope, believing that there is no way out. Now there is a pandemic that brings up all these feelings and fears for most of the population. Overwhelm and despair are common symptoms of a life tsunami, and we find ourselves drowning. We can't touch bottom, we are tired, we are barely staying above the water to breathe. It feels dark, damp, without light. The problem seems so hopeless and overwhelming. And sometimes it is not just one problem; sometimes multiple things hit us at the same time.

My last tsunami started with my mother passing away. Two weeks later, I lost my job of twenty-eight years. A week later my fiancé of seven years broke off the engagement. How did I get here? Is there a way out? Is it worth it to get out? It was total despair! It felt as though I was totally knocked down, and every time I tried to lift my head, another major tsunami would hit and knock me down again. Having gone through this, what I would like to share with anyone going through it right now in their life is that the first step is to know the truth. Not only is this *not* the end, but it is the rebirth of a new you!

When you are in the tsunami, when you hit bottom, this is as bad as it gets. But know that this is not all there is. After every big storm there is a rainbow, and so it is with you. There is a "best there is," and the best is just around the corner for you. What you are going through is just your journey; it is your life. This is a gift. You have been given a gift called Life. There is only one of you. You are so very important, and your contributions to this world are imperative to the well-being of all. When you are at the bottom, you are in despair, sad, angry, trapped, convinced there is no way out. Just know that not only is there a way out of the dark, there is a life waiting for you that is full of purpose, joy, abundance, and transformation.

There are two things that are needed in this stage--a desire to be uplifted, and the wisdom to know that there are worlds of wonder and fulfillment waiting for you. Your past is not your future. I can tell you with certainty that you will not only be okay, you will be a stronger and greater version of yourself. The most important thing is to know that it is not the end. It is important to know that this is only part of the process and amazing things are waiting for you.

The greatest thing about life is that every single day, every single moment gives us the opportunity to start over. What is keeping us trapped is our mind, our beliefs, our thoughts. How we spend the next minute can change the chain of events. How can we remove the darkness? By knowing that having light is possible.

In order to be uplifted, we must be able to feel the current pulling us toward the uplifting spiral. How did you get here? Sometimes it is something I call a "contradiction." It feels like what we are receiving is the opposite of what we wanted.

Actually, what we are receiving is exactly what we need to grow into what we desire.

When you ask for something with all your heart, it comes to you. For example, imagine being in kindergarten and wishing you were in high school. And imagine a genie giving you that wish. In order for a child to handle high school, they must go through growth (physical, emotional, spiritual). Sometimes the overwhelm that we are feeling is the growth that we need quickly in order to get us where we wish to be. It is actually a blessing, even though we are feeling overwhelmed and in despair. It is so important that through this process we are grateful that the Universe is moving us toward our desires.

We must be open to shifting all the thoughts that we have that bring us into despair. Our old thoughts may be true, but there is a possibility that they may not be true anymore. Maybe they were true yesterday, but they may not be true right now. What if these very thoughts that feel true, these thoughts that cause you so much suffering, are not as solid as they feel? If the pain level is high, it means you have been here for a long time. The pain seems to increase as we stay stuck. This is the way the Universe tells us that it is time for change. There is no reason to be stuck any more. The first steps of spiraling upward will feel difficult. Your energy may be so drained that any process will be difficult. There is a way out.

The First Step to the Way Out

If something is causing you pain, it is time to step back, identify your fears, and catch your thoughts. Fear can bring about emotional paralysis, and negative thoughts can become very painful. The first step is to acknowledge our fears and our thoughts. I know I am asking you to do something very difficult. The protector in you, your inner voice, is telling you to stay away from those thoughts. "Don't think them, ignore them, fight them, push them back, or even just let them be." Why would anyone acknowledge thoughts that hurt so much and you wish you didn't have in your life? The thoughts that are causing you pain are already in your life, whether you acknowledge them or not. Resisting them has not made them go anywhere. They are still there. Under the Chapter on Universal Laws, there is the Law of Action that says, **"What you resist, persists."** So whatever we are resisting, let's acknowledge it, and begin the journey of letting it all go.

Fear and Negative Thinking

Fear is a habit, so is self-pity, defeat, anxiety, despair, hopelessness, and resignation. You can eliminate all of these negative habits with two simple resolves: I can and I will.
—*Napoleon Hill*

Napoleon Hill viewed fear as a negative habit. Most of our fears are "False Evidence Appearing Real." Although our fears feel very real, they are just a memory. Fear is sometimes triggered by a memory, something undesirable that has happened in the past, as our mind believes will reoccur in the future. Other times fear is something undesirable that is happening that we wish was not happening. Fear sometimes becomes a habit that comes up so strong, it puts us into total emotional paralysis.

Today a few friends and I were discussing our greatest struggles with the Coronavirus, COVID-19. It was amazing how many of us had experienced the same thing. At the onset of the virus, as we were directed to stay home, so many of us experienced inertia. We had no energy to do anything, to work on anything. The fear of the virus was so overwhelming that nothing else could enter our awareness. Turning on the TV, listening to the radio, just immersed us deeper into the fears. COVID-19 was inescapable on TV. Every channel seemed to only talk about the virus. And for about two weeks, the only information provided was numbers. Deaths were reported like sports scores. We did not want this to be happening because we worried about ourselves, our loved ones, and everyone else in the world.

In the same discussion, we started talking about things we have been doing during the social distancing and stay-at-home order that bring us joy. There were so many great stories of people now having the opportunity to do things they love, spend time with their families, start projects at home, read books, cook with family, exercise. My gratefulness journal was overflowing with gratitude for spending time with my son, for the opportunity to spend time writing. Time on Zoom with friends was more special now as we missed seeing everyone in our life.

The most important way to surpass any fear is through the practice of gratefulness. Everything has two sides, a positive and a negative. Feeling grateful about anything takes you away from the past and the future and brings you in the present. Your gratefulness gives your mind the ability to move past the fear and grasp onto good things that are happening and things that you wish to attract into your life.

Below are some practices that will help us get out of the "hitting bottom" stage.

1.   Let's start by writing down the thoughts and beliefs that are causing you this pain.

2.   Acknowledge them calmly. Tell them, "I see you in my life!" If you are courageous, you may even say, "Welcome!!"

3.   Focus on your pain and try to locate it. Sometimes the pain is concentrated. You may be feeling it in your chest, your throat, your stomach. Most of the time I can feel a ball of energy stuck in my throat.

You may use one of the following exercises to blast the ball of pain.

Zapping Exercise

Close your eyes and concentrate on the ball of pain. Continue to focus on it, and especially focus on its center. You should experience a release, a break, a lessening of the pain. You can continue "zapping/focusing" the center of the pain until it is gone. If you cannot feel it in your body, don't worry. See the pain in your mind's eye and continue with the exercise of zapping its center. Approach this calmly and lovingly. Don't resist it, just lovingly focus on it. Most of the time we avoid our pain. As a result, it stays intact and keeps growing as we run the loop of negative thoughts about the situation.

The solution is to acknowledge it and get to the center of its intensity. If you cannot handle focusing on your pain at this stage, you may do an alternate exercise.

Alternate Exercises

1. Take a pen, look at it, and place all the energy of these thoughts and the pain in the pen.

2. Ask yourself, "Am I ready to let it go?"

3. Pick up the pen and drop it with intention to the floor. Even if the answer is "No, I am not ready to let it go," just by asking, some of the intensity of the pain should evaporate. Keep repeating this process, dropping the pen, and keep asking the question until the intensity is minimized. This should only take a few minutes.

If this is also too difficult to do, you may start with just a smile.

1. Smile as much as you can throughout your day. If this is difficult to do, lightly bite on a pencil (or pen). This puts you in a smiling pose when doing it naturally is difficult.

2. Release and keep doing this every day, until you begin seeing the problem minimize.

The reason I ask you to smile through this process is that it is difficult to have negative thoughts when you are smiling. I know that it may even be difficult to smile when you are in this state, but just try. Smile throughout the day as much and as long as you can. This is the first step.

Why This Works

When we are going through a tsunami in our life, our pain feels like it is chasing us. We keep running, trying to get away from it, and the more we run the more it chases us. At some point we will be out of breath from running and give up. The alternative is to get enough strength and energy to face it. Imagine chasing someone and suddenly they stop and start coming toward you, ready to confront you. You may not want to chase them anymore. As a matter of fact, you may start running away from them! The concept is the same. We must face our problems and zap them. Think of the witch in the Wizard of Oz, who melted when she was confronted and hit by water. In this case, you will hit the problem with your mind power, your focus.

Your Inner Voice

With many of the exercises in the book you will hear your inner voice. It will tell you that this will not work for you and that you should not even try these practices. It will tell you that your problems are unique; they are not like anyone else's. Your inner voice will tell you that no one understands your issues; you are alone. It will tell you that it is not possible to take your problems and put them in a pen like it is suggested. It will tell you it is crazy to acknowledge your pain, as pain is something to run away from. It is a waste of time. Your inner voice may even tell you that other people can do it, but you can't.

Always agree with your inner voice. "You are right, it was ridiculous and crazy in the past, but today I would like to give this a try." If you have difficulty with this and your inner voice tells you, "You see, I told you that you couldn't do it," just agree. Answer that you couldn't do it before, but you can now. Smile, and try again.

Your inner voice is trying to protect you; it is trying to stop change. In the caveman days, change meant danger. Some of our inner voice protective devices come from a primal time. It is all there for good reason. In order for you to move forward with your life, you need to give your inner voice an explanation so it may allow you to move forward. Sometimes agreeing and saying it was true yesterday, but today is different is a good way to bypass the protector, the inner voice.

Ideas to Ponder

There are several things that this process will make you realize. The most important is that your problems are separate from you.

- You are not your problems. You and all the problems you have are separate entities from the true "you." When you symbolically place them in the pen, you will see that you can bring them close, and you can move them away. They are not you.

- Although it may not feel like it, you are in control. You may also begin realizing that even with your inner voice, you must begin going with the flow, you must stop arguing with what is or what has been. What you resist persists. For example, if you tell yourself to stop thinking about the color red, you will find that all you will do is think of the color red. If you try to stop yourself from thinking of your car or your dog or anything at all, you will find that all you will do is think of whatever you are trying to resist. You see, what you resist persists.

- The only way to move beyond your inner voice is to agree with it and use the three dimensions: the past, the present, and the future. You can agree that this is what you did in the past but, beginning right now and in the future, something else will happen.

- The greatest thing is that every moment of the day we can change the future. Everything we do has a ripple effect. When we do good things for ourselves and others, good things happen. Unfortunately, the opposite is also the same. Every day is a new day, and every minute is a new minute.

- What keeps us a prisoner is when we keep thinking we are trapped. We must be aware of our thoughts. If they are thoughts of despair, we must acknowledge them and be willing to let them go. We must be aware that negative thoughts not only run on a loop, an endless repetition, but they also expand. Then we are stuck. But every minute we have the opportunity to look at things differently.

- If your current thinking does not work for you, the first step is to change your thinking. And I know it is not easy! We must be very gentle with the way we approach this. This can be by beginning with small steps--one smile, one negative thought that you welcome in your mind and then dismiss, one thought that yes, you can change your tomorrow.

- Remember, where you are right now is only temporary; all you need is the will to move yourself upwards just a little and the knowledge that where you are right now is the lowest you can be. Now it's time to start moving up. Notice that what you thought was "you"—all your beliefs and all your thoughts—are actually separate from the True You.

Chapter 2

Then, There Was Light

And the day came when the risk to remain in a tight bud was
more painful than the risk it took to blossom.
—Anais Nin

When you feel that some of the pain has evaporated and some of the heaviness is gone, you have now experienced your first upward spiral. It is like a wave that comes and carries you from the deep ocean toward the shore. You are still in water, but now your feet can touch ground. Now we are in a position to swim more securely and push ourselves toward the shore. You are not under water anymore.

It is like moving from the basement of a building to the first floor. You are beginning to feel the energy of the outside world. When you move from the basement to the first floor, now you have a window!! The window allows you to have light and to look at the street in a unique way. You get to hear the traffic, you get to see the piece of paper flying in the wind because someone threw it in the street. You get to see the people and their faces when it is hot, cold, crowded. You can see the homeless and the rich, the designer clothes and the torn clothes. You can see the good, bad, and the suffering. You can easily choose to be part of it; you can easily choose to be in it. Or you can choose to just be an observer.

Filters

This first floor gives you easy access to the street, and you can enter the picture any time you want. What you see in the outside world is your perception based on the filters you have accepted and believed. The filters make your emotions and beliefs more intense. You experience all of life through these filters, your very own lenses, your rose or gray (or you pick the color) glasses.

A very simple example: One day my friend was over at my house, and I had bought a cheesecake that had multi-flavored pieces. I asked my friend what piece he wanted. He looked at the box and said, "Chocolate." As I was serving, we continued our conversation about different topics. In the middle of the discussion he said, "No, I changed my mind, I want the Snickers-flavored piece."

Although I heard him—we were talking and I was distracted—by mistake, I gave him chocolate, his initial choice. As he took one bite he said, "You gave me the wrong piece of cheesecake!" I apologized and gave him the Snickers piece. As he started eating it, he continued to tell me how people never give him what he wants. Then he looked at me and said, "You also never want to give me what I want."

He believes that people do not want to give him what he wants. This is his filter. This filter is so strong, that even as he was eating what he wanted, he still believed he did not have what he wanted, and that people in general (including me) don't want to give him what he wants.

I could have spent a lifetime explaining how I wanted to give him what he wanted. I wanted him to be comfortable and have a great time in my home, but it would have been in vain. Once a belief is set, it is very difficult to convince someone that they are experiencing something different. Apologizing did not work. He was judge and jury; in his eyes I was guilty and there was no possibility that it really was a mistake for which I was very sorry.

Where do the filters come from? Sometimes our filters come from conclusions we have made about how life works based on our knowledge and experience. Other filters come from people who teach us and people we trust. Our parents teach us things that come from their filters. When our teachers and our friends talk about their pain, which shapes their filters, it shapes our filters as well. Our belief system has many layers created by our filters as well as others' filters. We must take a step back and question things, especially things that are hurting us, and examine the filter that has created them.

The Five Monkeys–Filters from Others

The experiment of the five monkeys illustrates how others' filters can impact our beliefs and our lives. In a large cage there are five monkeys. At the top of their cage there are bananas that can be reached easily through a ladder that is in the cage. When the first monkey starts climbing up the ladder, the experimenter soaks him and the four other monkeys with water using a hose. When a second monkey tries to go up the stairs to get to the bananas, the experimenter once again sprays the monkey with water, along with the other four monkeys. At this point one of the original monkeys is taken out of the cage and a new monkey is introduced in the cage. As the new monkey starts climbing the ladder, the other four monkeys pull him down and start beating him up. Again, the experimenter takes out a second monkey from the original set and replaces him with a new monkey. The second new monkey begins to climb the ladder and once again all the monkeys pull him off and start beating him, including the monkey that never experienced being sprayed with the hose!

We all learn things from our experiences, but we also learn from what others tell us (and sometimes beat us up about) and their experiences. What we have to keep in mind is that whatever we think we know as truth may no longer be true. And especially, we must be extra careful of things we learned indirectly. Others teach us things from their filtered view. If we believe them, we will believe things that just may not be true any longer. Consider that things may have changed. Question everything, and don't be afraid to dare to do things that others challenge. No one ever discovered something great without opposition. Challenge yourself, and challenge all your beliefs.

The Issue with Food—Filters from Experience

My father was in the city of Athens, Greece, during World War II. During the war, he witnessed hunger, as food was sparse. He went hungry, his brothers and sisters ate just enough to survive (he came from a family of sixteen children), and he witnessed people he knew die from starvation. Throughout his life my father would always buy extra canned goods and store them in case of another war. Even when we came to the United States this continued. My father built cabinets in our basement where he would put canned goods and pasta just in case. We all went along with this, as you could see the trauma he had experienced when he was much younger. Before he passed away, no food could ever be thrown away. Everyone had to eat all the food on his plate, or we would hear a story from the war. Sometimes my mother would have to secretly throw away food that had expired. Although the war was over many years before I was born, its effect on my father never went away. Every belief we have, every belief someone else has taught us, and every belief that activates our inner voice needs to be questioned.

As I am writing, this the world is going through the Coronavirus pandemic. The United States has declared a State of Emergency, and everyone is encouraged to stay home to reduce the spread of the virus. Yesterday I went to the supermarket because my refrigerator was just serviced, and for a couple of weeks my son and I had to throw out and consume almost everything that was in the refrigerator and freezer. As I walked into the superstore, I was stunned to see people in panic emptying the shelves. I was shocked to see there were no eggs in the store; there were no frozen vegetables and very few fresh vegetables. I found myself buying things I didn't need just because it was there. For an hour, I found myself joining in the energy and chaos of all that was going on. I was thinking about my father and wondering if this crisis will cause us as a country and as a world to worry about food. Will this become our lifetime filter? It is making me realize how we must all become centered and continue to follow our daily practices in order to become exempt from the fear and the chaos.

Let's ask ourselves, "Is the information that comes to us positive?" My son loves to watch the news every night. I often have to walk away, as everything is always presented with a negative spin, even the weather! When it used to snow in the 1960s, 1970s, 1980s, 1990s, the weather report would just predict snow. Now it is conveyed as though something is wrong, even when it is in the middle of winter. Every temperature now is compared to some average. We are told that whatever temperature it is outside, it should either be colder or hotter, according to this average. It is conveyed as though there is something wrong, and this could make people feel powerless and fearful.

I get my weather from Alexa these days. She seems to just tell me what is predicted for my location, without any judgment. Do what you need to do to keep things positive in your life, and stay away from things that present negativity that may not be true for you; it may just be someone else's perspective and journey. Protect yourself from negativity, and don't let it become your filter.

As we are going through the Coronavirus pandemic, I see how difficult this is. Every form of communication seems to be about the pandemic. Every communication predicts the worse. Whoever you speak to wants to talk about this, and the stories that people are projecting are based through negative filters. It is so important to protect yourself not only physically, but emotionally and spiritually. Do what the authorities say to stay safe. At the same time, know that the negative messages, when believed, will bring more of the same. Keep in your mind the picture of a healthy world, one that now has the wisdom to make it a loving, peaceful, and safe place to live.

The Golf Club—the Upward Spiral

A famous golf pro was invited by the royal family of Saudi Arabia to play golf with the king for the weekend. The golf pro accepted. He was picked up from his home by a limousine and brought to the airport where he boarded a private jet that flew him to Saudi Arabia. He was brought to the palace and treated like royalty. He met the king and his family and went out to a weekend of golf, elaborate food, elaborate everything.

At the end of the weekend, the golf pro could not believe the amazing weekend he had and how grateful he was to the king and his family for their kindness and hospitality. He didn't know how to express his gratefulness. To his surprise, the king came to him and told him what a great time he and his family had and told him that he wanted to give him a gift. Anything he wanted would be his. The golf pro explained that a gift was not necessary. As a matter of fact, he didn't know how to express his gratitude for the amazing weekend. The king insisted, so in order to comply, he said, "If you must give me something, I collect golf clubs. You may give me a golf club."

He flew back to the US, and for weeks he was trying to imagine what this club would look like. What if it was made of gold? How unique would it be coming from the king? Would it have diamonds all over it? The days and weeks went by. He kept looking at his mailbox expecting a long box with a club in it, but nothing. So many months went by that he forgot about it, thinking that the king had forgotten. Then one day in his mailbox was a large envelope from the king. When he opened it, he realized it was a deed to a five-hundred-acre golf club in America!

To a king, a golf club is a grand, beautiful place where people gather to play golf, socialize, and collaborate with others who are of similar social ranks and interests. To a golf pro, it is the instrument that you play golf with. Depending on your filter, the world is different. This difference determines your life experience.

Life will give you what you expect of it. If your view is small, this is what life will serve you. If your view is grand, this is what will come your way. Expect good things in your life. (We will be discussing this more in the chapter about Vision.) If you believe, "I never win anything," "I never get any breaks," "I never have any luck in life," then your life will be very different than if you turn all these statements positive. "I am a winner in life," "God always sends me blessings," "the Universe brings me only good things," "I am so fortunate," "I am so grateful." The grandness and vibration of your expectations will attract things that match that vibration.

The Filter Effect and Groundhog Day

Be aware of your filter. This is how sometimes we create the Groundhog Day syndrome. If you have seen the movie *Groundhog Day*, you remember the main character wakes up in the same day every day. He does not like this day and tries everything he can to stop waking up on this day without success ("what you resist persists!"). Even after killing himself (and the groundhog), the next day he wakes up again in Groundhog Day.

Some found the movie boring; some found it frustrating. The whole time the movie was showing us what happens in our life. When we do not resolve issues, when we are not aware the importance of letting go, the importance of the vibration we are emitting into the world, our issues will keep repeating in our lives until we resolve them.

Imagine having a belief that "no one gives me what I want." This can be a very painful mantra to have repeated in your life. Every time it is repeated in your life, it is another opportunity to let it go. Imagine all the other feelings and beliefs associated with this mantra. The belief that no one can be trusted, the belief that everyone is trying to hurt you are beliefs that cannot be let go very easily. When we hold a belief, we begin defending it and living our life as though it is true.

Sometimes we may not want to let go of our beliefs. Once we have a belief, we begin attracting situations in our lives that prove it to be true. People listen to our stories about how this belief is true and as a result may even feel sorry for us and try to be nicer to us and give us a break. The storyteller and the victim within us receive a level of enjoyment from this. It gets us attention and makes us feel good for a moment. As we keep repeating these stories, more people listen and feel sorry for us. Therefore, we now want to hold on to this belief even longer, so we can tell more people how we are victimized by others while our actions are attracting the same situations over and over in our lives.

It's like grabbing a poisonous snake by the neck that is trying to bite us and not letting it go because of the attention it brings us. And even when it bites us over and over again, we still do not let it go. Now multiply that by the number of poisonous beliefs we carry. Imagine multitudes of poisonous snakes biting us, but we refuse to let them go. Let's acknowledge that sometimes we enjoy the attention we get as a result of the stories. Our negative beliefs have served their purpose, but now let's be open to letting them go.

The Problem with Filters

Since so much of these processes take place in the subconscious mind, many of us often are not aware of some of our beliefs and filters. A good check is to look at what shows up in our lives. Everything that is in our lives can be traced back to our thoughts, beliefs, and filters. When you see something in your life that you wish was not there, it is time to question whether it is a contradiction that will get you to a place you have desired, or whether it is triggered by a negative belief or filter.

How do we know if a filter or belief is negative? You can assess it by checking it against Universal Laws. Does it promote love and unity? Does it promote abundance, health, joy, well-being for all?

When we become aware of a filter, we should question it. A good way to do this is to follow Byron Katie's process called The Work. Start by asking two questions: "Is it true?" and "Can you absolutely know that it's true?" This process helps us play with our thoughts and beliefs, and we often find that what we are struggling with may not even be true.

Imagine having a beach ball that is filled with filters, thoughts, and beliefs. This includes some of our thoughts and beliefs that create serious upsets for us with situations and with people in our lives. We believe that the beach ball is attached to our hand. Questioning our beliefs through this process is like realizing all the things that upset us are separate from us. We can play with the ball of our beliefs and even have fun with it.

Turning the thought around highlights how our filters and beliefs are separate from who we are. Questioning our beliefs and our filters gives us a new perspective. It broadens our world. Imagine if you believed the world is made up of one floor and then you discover it is a high-rise building with an unlimited number of floors. The more we open our mind and free ourselves from the stories, the filters, the beliefs that do not serve us, our world expands. We move up to a higher floor where we get to see more of the world, more order and beauty. As we move up, we experience a transformation that moves us toward our greatness, our purpose, the best version of ourselves.

Ideas to Ponder

- Your world is seen through your filter. Unfortunately, most times this is a filter of pain. Other times it may be a filter of others' pain that you believed. Your beliefs are a filtered and complicated network of knowledge and experiences with conclusions that may have been true in the past but may not be true for your present or your future.

- Some beliefs and experiences will be relived and repeated in your life until you break the chain.

- Question your beliefs and start identifying your filters. If you would like to change your current situation, you must be ready to let go of beliefs and filters that do not serve you.

Chapter 3

Understanding Self

Self, Meet Self

Everyone most likely is familiar with the story of Adam and Eve. Some people believe the story literally (after all, it is in the Bible). Others believe it is a symbolic story, one that is conflicting, especially when we try to judge it. Was eating the fruit Adam's fault, or was it Eve's fault? What made them do it? People have a lot to say about this story.

One Sunday, a group of young adults and I were discussing the story when it took on another meaning for me and the others participating in the discussion. As we were discussing Adam and Eve, it became confusing as to which version of Adam and Eve we were discussing. The story presents two versions. There is a first version of Adam and Eve, before the fruit of the tree of knowledge of good and evil and the snake. Then there is a second version of Adam and Eve after the fruit incident. In the first version, Adam and Eve live with the light of God and obey God. The second version reflects the loss of the light as they partake the fruit from a tree that God clearly had instructed them to not to.

If Adam and Eve represent us, do we also have two versions? Let's call our first version our True Self. Let's call the second version our Human Self.

Our True Self

In the first version of Adam and Eve, before the fruit, Adam and Eve seem to live in the light and presence of God. There is peace; there is love; there is eternity, joy, and abundance of everything. Adam and Eve are connected with God; they are an extension of God as they were both just created by God. A perfect God that has just created a perfect universe and perfect people. Adam and Eve, prior to the fruit incident, experience joy, happiness, connectedness with God, creativity, abundance, eternity. This is their true self, their true nature. There are no worries, no problems; there is no pain; there is no lack; there are no health issues; there is no death. This is home; this is Paradise.

We understand the importance of experiencing joy, happiness, connectedness with God, abundance, health, eternity because as humans we always aim to experience this. We seem to be seeking the state of being that Adam and Eve had before the fruit.

Throughout this book, I reference your "true self." For the purposes of an easy definition, this is it. Adam and Eve's experience every day before the fruit: the love, abundance, joy, happiness, health, eternity, total connectedness with God;

this is the "true self" experience. This is the easiest way to understand "true self."

What if this pre-fruit version of Adam and Eve is you? Can you close your eyes and experience this? Can you remember your "true self?" At any given time, each one of us is experiencing either our "true self" experience or our "human self" experience. When I tell people, "You are love; you are abundance; you are joy; you are health; you are eternal," they normally say, "Yes, I am." We all know that this is what we are at our core. We are spiritual beings that for one hundred years or so get to have a human experience. Yet most of us identify more with the human self than our true self, our spiritual self. The next chapters explore first our human self and then the journey toward finding our "true self."

Our Human Self

Although Adam and Eve lived peacefully before the fruit, we see the opposite after the fruit incident. Our human self can be associated with the "after the fruit" version of Adam and Eve. After the fruit, they entered the world of needs, of worry, of pain. At first, we see them hiding as they suddenly realize they are naked. The first need we see in Adam and Eve was the need for clothes. Let's explore our needs, as they seem to be key in understanding our human self.

The Needs Filter

One of the basic "needs" theories was presented by Abraham Maslow. Maslow describes our upward spiraling needs of

Physiological (food, water, shelter), Safety (feeling safe and secure), Belonging (our relationships and friendships), Esteem (our need to achieve and accomplish), and Self-Actualization (achieving our full potential). When we look at our human self, we can see that many of our decisions and many of our choices are based on our needs. Much of the human drama is triggered by people feeling lack in any of the above areas as they progress in Maslow's hierarchy of needs.

When we make decisions based on needs, we often lack clarity and may make decisions that fulfill a need but will not necessarily fulfill our life purpose. We may take a job we don't like in order to meet physiological needs. We may spend a lifetime trying to get others to approve of us to meet our need of belonging. I have friends who have bought houses they could not afford for the esteem of living in a high-end area or to get approval.

One of the top releasing programs, The Sedona Method, can link most human needs to five areas: the need to give or receive approval, the need to control or be controlled, the need for security, the need for separation, and the need for oneness. With all needs we find that our ego has taken over and fear is at the bottom of our actions. When I find that my actions are linked to one of these needs, then it is time to release.

Many times, especially when there is struggle, our ego is involved. In many theories, our ego is correlated with human suffering and pain. However, the ego is part of who we are. Since we must embrace all of who we are, we must also embrace our ego. Without our ego we could not understand our human self, or the human nature in others. Understanding our ego takes some introspection. It is just something we need to keep in check. Most of the times when my feelings are hurt, it is my ego. The times when I have made an assumption that is just not true, it is normally my ego.

The Feeling Filter

As we discussed before, how we see the world and how we experience our life is dependent on our filters. In addition to the "needs" filter, as humans we get to experience feelings. Our feelings drive our life experiences. There are positive feelings which include love, joy, peace, enlightenment, interest, wonder. There are also negative feelings such as fear, anger, grief, guilt, and so on.

When it comes to our feelings, often we get to experience a feelings progression. We may experience guilt, which if not handled properly may eventually lead to fear and anger. Our positive feelings work the same way.

Our feelings create vibrational frequencies, which play a huge part in our ability to attract experiences in our lives. Below you will find Dr. David Hawkins's "Map of Consciousness" that reflects positive and negative feelings, as well as the frequencies they emit. These are in rank order. Notice that if we are feeling shame or guilt, and this progresses to fear, we are actually moving up in frequency.

Our emotional vibrational frequencies are measured in hertz. As we react to different situations, our vibration changes as our emotions change. A vibration analysis could show you your frequency in a specific situation. If you see someone who has hurt you in the past, you may find yourself automatically reacting at a grief, fear, or anger level. This will bring your vibrational frequency down. You may choose to override this by reacting with courage, acceptance, or even peace.

If this is difficult for you to do, you may use the releasing techniques that are described later in the book, or you may meditate or even do neuro-linguistic programming to reprogram your responses. The key is self-awareness, keeping track of your feelings and emotions, and knowing that you are able to adjust them and bring them to a higher level.

You will also notice that the lower-frequency emotions are associated with the ego, whereas higher up the chart are the spiritual, inspirational emotions as you reach the ultimate state of enlightenment.

Map of Consciousness (with Frequency Level)

Enlightenment (above 600 Hz)		
Peace	600	
Joy	540	
Love	500	
Reason	400	
Acceptance	350	
Willingness	310	
Neutrality	250	
Courage	200	
Pride	175	
Anger	150	
Desire	125	
Fear	100	
Grief	75	
Apathy	50	
Guilt	30	
Shame	20	

Try to stay above 200 Hz

The longer we can stay in a vibration of higher than 200, we will be moving toward experiencing joy, peace, and enlightenment. As like attracts like, the more we are able to stay in a positive frequency (above 200) the more positive things we can attract into our lives. As such, we must keep our feelings in check (More on this in the later chapters of this book.)

Although we may feel we have no control over our feelings, we actually do. As we are energy beings, our energy is emitted out into the world. You can see this when a positive person walks into the room, and you feel the energy level of the room rise. At the same time, if someone with negative energy frequency walks into the room, the energy level drops. We must stay aware of how we are feeling at all times, and we must do things that will help us stay in a positive vibrational frequency.

For example, in the book *How to Win Friends and Influence People* by Dale Carnegie, you will note that the very first principle is "Don't Criticize, Condemn, or Complain." This is only one way that we can avoid lowering our frequency. When we are feeling down, watching the news, or even talking to a friend and complaining about others or situations in the world, it will bring our frequency down even more.

Being stuck in a negative frequency brings us pain. We hold on to the anger toward someone, and that becomes toxic within us. According to Louise Hay, if we look at the root cause of all illnesses, we will find an emotion. Negative emotions hurt us more than they hurt anyone else. It is said that holding onto resentment, anger, or hate is like taking poison and expecting someone else to die. We must find ways to release negativity in our journey toward our greatness and keep ourselves in a state of high vibrational energy and positive thinking. (More on how to do this in the Law of Attraction chapter.)

Versions of Ourselves

Just like software upgrades come with new versions, the same happens with people. Both at the "true self" spiritual level, as well as the human level, there is expansion and transformation. New versions of yourself emerge. At the spiritual level, there is a continual expansion of love. As we experience life, our ability to love and our ability to know God expands. As this expansion takes place, we expand as loving beings.

Our human self also transforms. As time goes by, we can look back at any time and clearly see old versions of ourselves.

There are versions of myself I remember clearly. Then there are versions of myself that seem foreign to me. I know certain things happened. I know how I reacted. I have all the excuses and stories, but it feels like the person who reacted that way could never have been me. The version of myself in my twenties and the version of myself now, one may consider as different people. There is always an earlier version of ourselves that didn't know what we know now.

Through the years, through our tsunamis, through our tough times, we evolve. Some of the things that happened in the past could be viewed as mistakes, but I know they weren't. They were me living with less knowledge and experience. We need to embrace all these versions of us, and we also must embrace all the events, including the tsunamis, that led us to today and our current version. The amazing you of today is a result of all that has happened. If we take any of those events, experiences, even traumas away, then you would not be you. Love yourself just as you are and move forward with your life.

There have been some communications with my ex-fiancé as he asks why things happened as they did. That relationship ended twelve years ago. Sometimes when I think back, all I feel is compassion for that version of me whom I don't fully remember or understand any longer. I could go on and on with stories and drama of all that happened, but it is irrelevant. At that time, that version of me was going to put up with anything to be in a relationship and to be engaged and to be married to this man that I thought was truly amazing. If it wasn't for this man, I would never be writing this book. He expanded my world both physically with his love for adventure and spiritually. He introduced me to the realm of spirituality, and for that I will always be grateful.

When the day came that we broke up (for the last time) right after my mother had died, and right after I had lost my job, something drastically changed inside me. I came out of that phase of my life as a different person. This new version liked me, and that was a top priority over being in a relationship or being engaged or married. It took many years of self-reflection to understand that everything that had happened was perfect, and that all happened just as it should have.

You are you because of all that has happened in your life. We want to label everything as good or bad, but in reality, all the events in your life created the beautiful, wonderful YOU. Let's embrace all of it, let's understand that we grew, and we are still growing. Let's forgive our earlier versions of us because they just didn't know.

New Version of Yourself

When you face a tsunami, a transformation happens. This can only happen if you are not fixated on the past. It is said that transformation in people happens through challenges or through passionate desire to change.

Earlier I spoke of one of my tsunamis. First, my mother passed away. Then within two weeks I lost a job after twenty-eight years. Two weeks after that, my fiancé of seven years walked away from our relationship.

Although 2008 was the year of the triple tsunami, it was also one of the greatest years of my life! A new version of me emerged. What happened as a result of this new version? It was in 2008 that I got my job with British Telecom, one of the greatest companies on earth. It was that year that I was runner up in the Toastmasters International speaking competition (runner up as best speaker in New York and New Jersey). It was that year that I was recognized as being in the top ten percent of trainers in the global training organization that I was teaching in the evenings at the time. It was that year that I got to travel to the UK, Switzerland, Vancouver, and even went back to Greece after twenty years. My son received his associate's degree in 2008 and went on for his bachelor's degree.

Your worst year can become your best year if you change your thoughts, embrace your pain, trust in the Universe, become grateful for everything and everyone in your life, and allow your transformation. It is said that no one knows enough to ever be pessimistic, which is true. Where you are today has nothing to do with where you will be in the future. Who you are today may be unrecognizable in a very short time. Know that your journey is one of knowing your true self and liking yourself. Make it a goal to know yourself, stop criticizing yourself, and stop guilt.

All that you did in the past was based on that version of yourself, and it was based on what you knew then. Who you were in the past doesn't have to be who you are in the future, unless you choose to hold on to the past and that version of you. Your future holds fabulous, amazing miracles if you allow them to enter your life. I am hoping that every single one of my readers will find their way to the miracles, to the sacred flow, to happiness, to their purpose, to their greatness.

Ideas to Ponder

- As we live this life, it feels like there is only a human self.

- In reality, there are two versions within us: our human self and our true self.

- Our human self experiences life through our lenses of pain: ones we have experienced personally and ones we have believed from others.

- Our human self has filters based on our needs and also on our feelings.

- Being aware of our true self and especially knowing how to access our true self is a huge step in finding the peace, joy, health, love, abundance that we may be looking for.

- Our true self is all goodness and love.

- Our true self understands what is important and how the Universe works.

- We all have access to our true self and should learn to access it readily.

- Living at the level of our true self, we get to experience the love, joy, abundance, peace, happiness that we crave.

- Our true self is connected to God and emanates love toward self, others, and all things in the Universe.

- Since our human perceptions are based on needs, experiences of pain, and feelings, they are a flawed view.

- In our journey to the best version of ourselves, we evolve into many versions that normally are marked with life milestones, realizations, small steps of transformational greatness.

- A new version is created subsequent to:

  o Contradictions

  o Painful experiences

  o Spiritual understanding and expansion

Chapter 4

Falling in Love (with You)

In falling in love with ourselves, we must be aware of both our true self and our human self. When we discover our true self, it fills us with love toward ourselves, toward others, toward everything in the Universe. Falling in love with our human self is a tougher job. Within our human self lives our ego, which is a tough judge of everything. Imagine how different life would be if we loved ourselves. How would our world be different? Would we say bad things to ourselves? Would we treat ourselves differently? Would we believe others when they say bad things to us about us? Would we allow others to hurt us physically or emotionally?

Loving ourselves is so important to living life fully. If we don't like ourselves, attempting to like others becomes a difficult, energy-draining job. Everything becomes difficult. Fully contributing to the world and being happy becomes difficult. And in this state, we will attract others who don't like themselves and cannot truly love or fully contribute. Not liking ourselves puts us in a state of neediness. Our very ability to be happy is closely linked to liking ourselves.

My ex-husband used to tell me that we were a perfect match. He used to say that I like to give, and he likes to take. This makes us perfect for each other. I used to think "Well, how much could a taker take?" For people who don't like themselves, for those who are needy, for those who are "takers," it is never enough.

"Takers" never really appreciate what others do for them. However, I thought that by my giving more he would like me more. This is because I didn't like myself, and worse yet, I did not value myself. Notice that I didn't expect him to *love* me; I was giving just to be *liked*! At some level, I didn't think I deserved love. And although I didn't expect it, I would get upset with him for not loving me, for not respecting me, for taking from me, for being unfaithful.

If you don't like yourself, you find yourself in a forever cycle of neediness, never being satisfied, never getting what you need. You find yourself hurt mostly and also causing hurt to others. We receive love at the same level as we love ourselves. If we don't like ourselves, if we don't feel the love that is within us and surrounds us, regardless of what others do for us, it becomes a struggle to recognize it and feel happy. When I look at previous versions of myself, I am amazed at all the things I didn't know and didn't understand. I am amazed at how many times I gave away my power to others. I am amazed at how hard I worked and all I gave to get back what I didn't have to begin with.

If you are in a relationship where you find yourself compromised in order to keep the relationship going, please take a step back and look closer. The bravest thing to do is to step away until you sort things out. The most painful thing to do is to stay in the relationship where you get smaller and smaller, and you totally lose yourself and your self-esteem. Please take the time to reintroduce yourself to the amazing you!

I am not asking you to do something I have not done. I have stepped away from relationships. I have stepped away from a church, from clubs, from jobs that put me in a box and would not allow me to grow and be me. It doesn't mean you will step away forever; just until you make some agreements with yourself about how you will treat yourself, and how you will expect to be treated. I am also not telling you to step away with hate or resentment. Anything that comes into our lives that triggers our growth does not deserve resentment. Most of the time situations that challenge us trigger our growth and transformation, so understand the purpose of the challenge, understand the lessons and changes it triggered in your life, and be grateful for the new brilliant you.

When we lose ourselves, sometimes we must take a step back to remember just how valuable we are. It is like being homeless, yet there are millions of dollars in our bank account. Sometimes we compromise ourselves because we don't understand our worth. Why is it that we cannot see what we have within us? In teaching self-improvement courses, sometimes I wish people could see themselves how I see them. People's brilliance is so obvious. Even in knowing people for short timeframes as they take a course I teach or during a professional assignment, sometimes I am fascinated with how often we miss our own brilliance. Why is it that we can't see just how amazing we are and instead put up with abuse, disrespect, and things that hurt us?

It seems that at one time in life, when we were very young, we knew how amazing we were. But as years went by, we believed the illusions we heard and experienced. Every baby knows how beautiful they are. We, too, knew at one time. Yet as time went on, we believed judgments we heard about our looks and our abilities, and we convinced ourselves that we do not deserve good things unless we meet these made-up standards. We become our biggest critic and keep repeating these judgments. We tell ourselves that we must be perfect or else.

In my classes I ask, "If you were in kindergarten right now and I asked you to come up here and sing any song, how many of you would come up?" Almost every participants' hand would go up. Then I would say, "Who would like to come up and sing any song right now?" Normally one or two hands go up. What happened to us between kindergarten and now? For some of us it may have been that, as we were singing someone said, "Stop making that terrible noise!" For others, we may have seen the consequences when others put themselves out there in front of a crowd of people.

Our life seems to be a circular journey of knowing, forgetting, then ultimately remembering again. So let's remember now what we already know. Let's look at a few possibilities.

Is it possible that even if you are in a situation where others put you down, there is no one in this world more important than you are?

You are as important as anyone else in this world. Take care of yourself. Never believe anyone who tells you that you are less than anyone else. Think of the oxygen mask on the airplane. If the oxygen mask comes down, you are instructed to put yours on first, then put the mask on the children and others you are caring for. If you don't take care of you, others will suffer. Don't believe anyone who tells you that you are less important than anyone else. You cannot stop them from saying it, but you don't have to believe it. You are unique, you are a treasure, just as everyone else is unique and important.

Is it possible that you are absolutely beautiful/handsome?

Every person is beautiful. Just remember that beauty is subjective. Every culture has their own version of beauty. I spent most of my life not liking myself because my skin was light. My beautiful cousins in Greece were so dark and in the summer would always look like they were tan. I walked around with my legs looking white, and any attempt toward a tan would result in sunburn.

Surprisingly in teaching personal development courses, I discovered people who expressed that they didn't feel beautiful because they thought their skin was too dark. It was so confusing to me, but it led me to the realization that our body, our skin color, our size, our hair color, our eye color, or whatever else is making us think less of ourselves, is not what makes us beautiful. We just are.

Is it possible that you are so very smart?

You are so very smart. And you can do things that so many people cannot do. The song you write is your song, the book you write is only yours. Everything you do is something that has your special touch. Don't believe anyone who tells you otherwise, especially the little voice in your head.

By now you know what to do when your inner voice starts telling you lots of negative stories about you and what it may judge as the not-so-smart things that you may have done in the past. Tell your inner voice, "That was yesterday; now I am living in my brilliance."

All the Good Things You Deserve
Is it possible that you deserve love?

Love is the essence of the Universe. We not only deserve it; we are immersed in it. We are always loved and living in love. If you are not feeling loved, it just means that you are standing in a spot of life where you cannot see it. Just a little shift will make it all visible again. Please continue reading, as each step in this book brings you closer to your true self, the self without blind spots.

If we don't like ourselves, it becomes very difficult for others to fall in love with who we truly are. If we don't like ourselves, we bring forth someone other than the true us. We bring forth the person that we want others to see and love, not who we truly are.

The divorce rate in the US is high. So many people find themselves married to a different person than who they thought they fell in love with. This is because most of the time the person we brought to the relationship was not really us. In the beginning of the relationship, very often we compromise.

I am not an adventurous person, yet I was engaged to a wonderful man who loved adventure. I joined his world, and it was fantastic. After seven years, he couldn't understand why on long hikes I would ask if I could go sit under a tree or a bush and just read until he came back to get me. Many times, I could see that he wanted me to hike with him like I used to in the beginning of the relationship so we could experience nature together. But I got to the point where I couldn't do it anymore. He, too, had made many compromises, joining me in events that he didn't have any interest in; but again, a lifetime is a long time to compromise with these things.

We all deserve love. The best way to receive it is to put our true self forward, the self that is not needy or attached. As we are transformed and move up another step toward our greatness, we begin to attract the right people in our lives. These are people that will support us as we jointly evolve toward our greatness.

Is it possible that you deserve health?

We are all meant to be healthy. We can see how quickly our body reacts when we have a wound of any kind. Everything in our body moves toward healing the wound. The majority of our health issues are a result of worry, stress, and living a life of separation.

In her book, *You Can Heal Your Life*, Louise Hay lists every ailment and provides the beliefs and thoughts that cause it. She also provides affirmations for every ailment. I have personally used these affirmations and have also shared them with my closest friends. They help tremendously, but they are not a cure-all.

Our thinking and beliefs are a complicated process, and there are many layers. They do work in step with the Law of Attraction. I am hoping that you find the actions presented in this book simple to adapt into your life. I am hoping that you are well on your way to putting things in perspective, separating, and letting go of issues that cause stress and worry, as this is where many of our ailments live. There are more actions to come!

Is it possible that you deserve the best of everything?

We deserve the best of everything for ourselves and our families. We have been given the ability to accomplish anything we want to do. (If you don't know what you want to do, we will discuss that in the chapter about Purpose.) Sometimes what we want to do is buried under our fears, our judgments of ourselves, our judgments of others, and our holding on to the past. Let's fall in *like* with ourselves. Let's acknowledge how very special we are. There is only one *you* on this earth.

Don't Let Yourself (or Others) Put You Down

Many years after our divorce, my ex-husband—who lived in Greece with his new family—called me to ask if he could come back to the United States to stay with me and my son. He had left us when my son was only five years old, moved to Greece, and remarried. When he asked, all I felt was compassion, friendship, and pure love. He was going to stay with us for only two weeks, and I was more than happy to have him.

In the beginning everyone was polite and respectful. Then two weeks turned to one month, then two, then three, then four, then five months. Just like when we were married, I found myself paying for everything. He looked for jobs and worked intermittently. Just like when we were married, he drew comparisons and judgments between me and others in his life. He told me my house was not as nice as his friend's house. My cooking was not up to par to his new wife and others in his life. We had resumed our roles from when we were married, and he freely shared his negative judgments of me.

The greatest thing was that we were not married any more. Although I was reliving being the victim of the past, something was different. The version of myself that thought I had to endure words of judgment and criticism was long gone. This version knew that we were not married anymore! This version knew that the chains of a painful marriage had been cut fifteen years earlier! So one day while he was complaining that I was only doing the laundry once a week and that was not enough for him, he uttered the words, "That's it! I am leaving."

These were the words that most frightened me years ago when we were married. Back then, I truly thought I couldn't live without him. Back then I was willing to do anything in order for him to stay so we could be a family and raise our son. This time when I heard the words "That's it! I am leaving," I answered quickly and easily, "That would be fine. Please don't forget to leave behind the keys to the house and the car. Also, let's meet at the Verizon store tomorrow, because I will not be paying for your mobile phone any longer."

He was shocked. He went upstairs, packed, and left. It was one of the most liberating moments, because I could see how far I had come in my life. I wish I could go back and talk to myself of thirty years ago to tell her how okay it would be if he left. But you see, we can't do that. We must go through our journey and learn as we go. At any given time, we don't know what we don't know. And back then people in our lives didn't know what they didn't know. That's the reason we must release our past.

Reminder Exercise

1. Take a few minutes to write down things that you have done in your life that you are so very proud of.

    *   What skill(s) have you learned?

    *   What talents do you have?

    *   How many opportunities have you had the courage to say "yes" to?

    *   Remember the day you got your driver's license? What a huge accomplishment!

    *   Have you graduated from a school?

- Have you ever followed your heart, accomplished something you didn't think was possible?

- Have you made, fixed, or built something?

- Have you passed difficult exams?

Remind yourself that you are the same person who did those things! All the talents, skills, and courage that made you successful then are still within you. List these talents and skills within you, give them a name, and know these will spiral you into your next successful endeavor.

2. Take a few minutes to remember different versions of yourself and how you are different now in comparison to the version of yourself of many years ago. How are you different? What triggered these changes?

Introspection Exercise

1. Are there areas where you are stuck?

2. Can you identify areas of strength that the future version of you will have?

3. How different do you anticipate being? How will these differences help you in your future life journey and your life purpose?

Mirror Exercise

1. Look into a mirror every night, look into your eyes, and tell yourself "(Your name), I appreciate you for..." and fill in the blank.

    *   Tell yourself what you did that day that deserves appreciation.

    *   What did you achieve this day?

    *   What are you proud of today?

    *   Did you exercise, meditate, follow a healthy habit?

    Say it out loud. Then when you are done, look into the mirror, look into your eyes, and say, "(Your name), I love you."

    In the beginning, this exercise may be quite uncomfortable. Every day that you tell yourself "I love you," part of the wall begins to come down in the journey of liking and ultimately loving yourself. Don't let your inner voice take you out of this exercise. It gets easier with time.

2. It is so important that you stop saying anything negative about yourself. Catch yourself when you do. You can have the words "I am" be the alarm that wakes you up to listen to what follows. Any time you say, "I am," immediately follow it with a positive statement.

Loving yourself erases the many layers of blockage. It gives you the freedom to put forth your true self without apology or guilt. It gives you independence from other people's approval or disapproval. If you love yourself (without allowing your ego to take over), you are untouchable from anyone trying to control you or from the need to control others. Loving yourself gives you the ability to respect and love others. It gives you the capability to feel compassion for others, and it gives you the capability to feel the love that comes back to you.

The Alarms

I don't know about you, but I don't know what I would do without my alarms. I have one in the morning to ensure I make my seven a.m. calls on time with my colleagues in Europe. I have alarms throughout the day making sure I get on my conference calls at least five minutes early. I hear an alarm when a text arrives on my phone. There are sounds that come from everywhere, sometimes to tell me the coffee is ready, the dishwasher has completed its cycle, the clothes are dry.

And then there are personal alarms, the ones no one hears except me. Although they are not physical alarms, I jump when certain things happen to ensure that I redirect. I will mention three alarms that support me.

1. Negative thinking. When I realize negative thoughts have crept in, it is time to redirect.

2. "I am…" Whenever I say or think those two words, the alarm that goes off in my brain tells me that what follows should be positive.

3. "I can't…" Those words are also ones that make us a victim. Try replacing the words "I can't" with "I will not." Saying "I will not" or "I won't" shifts the energy from "I am a helpless victim" to "I am in charge of my life, and I choose not to do that."

If you are a person who has a tough time saying "no," you will find that this will be a tough one. You must know that you can do anything you put your mind to do. I have repeatedly proven this to myself.

In my forties, I bought a motorcycle and rode it exclusively. I did comedy. I still enter the Toastmasters International speaking competitions. Why do I do these things? To experience joy, and to remind myself that I can do anything.

Doing things you think you can't do changes your energy, expands your experiences, and brings you joy. You can live your life to its fullest. There will be things you will enjoy and things you will not. You will not know until you try. To your success, in all you do!!

Words of Caution

Many people have a serious issue with anyone telling them to "fall in love with yourself." They don't want to be this person who is arrogant and egotistical. To clarify, I am not asking you to be the person who walks in the room and declares, "I am better than everyone else here." I am not asking you to be the person that demands to be revered by others. What I am asking you to do is to acknowledge your perfection as a creation and extension of God. I am asking that you stop thinking negative thoughts about yourself. I am asking that you create a space for love in your life.

Your ability to love yourself and to feel loved are interrelated. If you don't love yourself, you can be flooded with love, but you will still feel like love is missing from your life. Loving yourself also expands your ability to love others. Be aware of your feelings, and be able to distinguish between love versus infatuation and love versus need. If you are reaching into the world from a perspective of need, you are bound to attract the wrong people into your life, and you are bound to stay in the relationship longer than you should.

Seeking Perfection

One of the ways we hurt ourselves and create struggle in our lives is by trying to be perfect. We want to be perfect because we or others have set standards for us that are difficult and often not reachable. We want to be perfect to get the approval of others. My advice is stop trying to be perfect. You already are, and let me share why.

First, whatever you have defined as an imperfection in yourself is actually part of what makes you perfect. If you believe the Divine Source, God, is perfect, then how could something perfect make something imperfect? How can we believe that everything in the universe has been created to be perfect, except people? Did God say, "I will make the birds to be perfect and the trees and the mountains and the oceans and all living things perfect—except people; I will purposely make them imperfect"?

Everyone and everything have been made perfect for their purpose in life. If you are not very good in math, if you are not good in literature and arts, if every teacher on this earth has told you how imperfect you are because you cannot do these things, maybe they have judged you with the wrong measure. I am convinced that those who have math in their life purpose are born with excellent math skills. Those who are supposed to write or sing or create beautiful art are born with those skills.

Why do we think we have to be good in everything? We were not meant to be good in everything. We were meant to have specific talents to do the things we love to do toward our purpose. Like Albert Einstein said, "Everybody is a genius. But if you judge a fish by its ability to climb a tree, it will live its whole life believing that it is stupid." What if the fish believed that it was a bad fish because it couldn't climb that tree? Fish are created to do what they are supposed to do.

Likewise, people are created with different skills and talents to fulfill their unique purposes. If you have judged yourself as too short, too tall, too fat, too skinny, too young, too old, not good enough, not smart enough, not strong enough, not educated enough, too educated, too hurt, too lazy, stop! Stop judging yourself, and go out there and do all the things you are fabulous at doing! You will bump into people who can fabulously do the things you can't do, while you can do things they could never do the way you do them. Love and honor the people that can do things you can't do. We are all here to be unique and complement each other.

The Girl and the Jug

There was a girl in a village who took her jug every day to the spring, filled it with water, and brought it back to her family. The jug had a crack in it. When she got to the spring, she would fill the jug with water. On her way home, drops of water would leak through the crack and fall onto the path. If someone looked at that jug, he would conclude it is not perfect because of the crack.

We may think we are not perfect. We are all very good at identifying all the cracks in ourselves. If we only look at the crack, we judge the jug and consider it to be so very flawed.

Yet if you look back at the path, you will see flowers growing all across this particular path. The water that falls from the jug waters the flowers every day and makes it the most beautiful path of all. We may focus on our cracks and judge them as imperfect and unacceptable. What we are not considering is the contribution of that crack, that we consider our imperfection, to the world. What we consider our flaws are sometimes our very perfection; They are what makes us unique. Only we are able to contribute to the world the way we do, cracks and all.

Ideas to Ponder

- We are made perfect for our life purpose.

- Everything we consider our imperfections are actually part of our perfection.

- We must learn to love ourselves and avoid negative feelings (especially guilt) in order to experience life fully.

- We deserve the very best life has to offer us; we deserve nothing less.

- We should set an alarm to redirect our thinking when we experience:

  o Negative thoughts.

  o We say or think the words, "I am…" (These words should always be followed by something positive.).

  o We say or think the words, "I can't…" (These words should always be substituted by the words "I won't.").

Chapter 5

Letting Others In

I see every person in my life as a true miracle. I think of how humans have been on earth for 200,000 years. Imagine all the synchronicity that had to take place in order for us to coexist with all the other human beings on this earth right now. And imagine the extra synchronicity that was needed in order to pass a particular person in the street or to have another individual in your meeting, your conference, your class. And yet imagine the additional serendipity of two people knowing each other deeply and interacting in this life. I have found that everyone comes into our lives to love us or to teach us something.

Every time I meet anyone, I view it as a miracle. I am so happy to meet them! I am so privileged to have them in my life, even the ones that left my life and left pain and trauma behind them. They were my teachers, and even those that meant to harm me actually contributed to my strength, spirituality, and ability to love. It all had a purpose, and although I didn't see it at that time, I see it years after. So now I know it is all for good.

All I can say is a huge "Thank you" to all who participated in my life and the evolution of me. To anyone I may have hurt inadvertently, I sincerely apologize and can only send love and blessings. I hope that God gives everyone the wisdom to understand what happened in their life and to see that it is all for good.

In the journey of liking yourself, letting others in becomes the lab. The roles people will play in your life will be the experiment. What I have found in my life is that when I didn't like myself, the people I let in validated all the reasons and stories and beliefs of why I did not deserve love, kindness, and positive things in my life. We can only experience the level of love that we have for ourselves, so when we don't like ourselves, we attract people who don't like us. The more we like and accept ourselves, the more we will experience that increased level of love from others. The people that enter and leave our lives will serve different purposes.

This poem describes it best:

People come into your life for a Reason, a Season, or a Lifetime. When you figure out which one it is, you will know what to do for each person.

When someone is in your life for a REASON,

It is normally to fill a need you have expressed. They have come to assist you through a difficulty; to provide you with guidance and support; to aid you physically, emotionally, or spiritually. They may seem like a godsend, and they are. They are there for the reason you want them to be. Then, without any wrongdoing on your part or at an inconvenient time, this person will say or do something to bring the relationship to an end. Sometimes they die; sometimes they walk away. Sometimes they act up and force you to take a stand. What we must realize is that our need has been met, our desire fulfilled; their work is done; The prayer you sent up has been answered, and now it is time to move on;

Some people come into your life for a SEASON,

Because your turn has come to share, grow, or learn. They bring you an experience of peace or make you laugh. They may teach you something you have never done. They usually give you an unbelievable amount of joy. Believe it. It is real. But only for a season.

LIFETIME relationships teach you lifetime lessons.

Things you must build upon to have a solid emotional foundation. Your job is to accept the lesson, love the person, and put what you have learned to use in all other relationships and areas of your life. It is said that love is blind, but friendship is clairvoyant.

-Author Unknown

This is such a great poem. It helps us understand and give closure to relationships that otherwise may bring up negative emotions. It makes me grateful for every person that has entered my life and the purpose they have served.

Mother Teresa, in her poem "Anyway" also reminds us that, regardless of who we may meet in our life journey, to remember that it is not about us and other people, it is always between us and God. When we take our last breath, all the judgments from others, or even people who have been dishonest, selfish, jealous, will not matter. So we must know to be kind and honest, to be forgiving, and to live our purpose, regardless of what others may say or do.

The Clay Buddha – A Different Way to See Others

During one of my trips to Asia in 1997, the way I look at people (and myself) totally changed. The temple of the Clay Buddha gives us a different view of people and who they truly are.

In 1955, there was a ten-foot statue of Buddha in Thailand that everyone believed was made out of clay. When it was time to move it to a new location, they discovered that they had underestimated its weight. Initially, believing the statue was made out of clay, they thought it could be moved by getting a few men to pick it up, place on a truck, and move it. It turned out that the statue was so heavy, it could not be picked up. Ultimately the statue was moved by a crane. In maneuvering it with the crane, the statue was dropped. That's when a monk saw that a piece of the clay had fallen off and noticed something shiny inside. When they scraped the clay off the Buddha, they realized that the Buddha was made of pure gold!

Looking at the Buddha, it looked like a light, movable, relatively cheap object. In reality, it was five and a half tons of pure gold. But in order to discover this, the monk had to look inside, he had to pay attention to what was beyond the clay in order to see the truth, the light, and the shine.

When people look at us, they only see what we choose to display. Some display poverty, homelessness, anger, hate. Others display a beautiful smile with beautiful clothes, beautiful homes, beautiful cars. Yet everyone is the same. We are all pure gold. Although we may choose to judge a stranger by their appearance, by their emotions, by their status in society, this judgment is flawed because all we see is the clay. What if we knew that underneath the clay we see is actually pure gold?

The principle of the Clay Buddha gives you x-ray vision into every person around you. Regardless of the ranting and raving of people, I now look in their eyes and only see the good. I acknowledge the good in them. Imagine if you only saw the gold in everyone. And I know, some people have so many layers of clay, it really takes a lot to get to that gold, but knowing it is there creates a different reaction. It is only a matter of finding it and reaching it.

There are many stories that reference this gold in people. Eckhart Tolle talks of the homeless man begging while sitting on a chest. He never opens or looks inside the chest. If he were to open it, he would find there are gold treasures inside. Are we all billionaires in who we are and yet act like we have nothing because we don't know our true self?

As I see the gold in people, I also see their potential. As I was teaching a professional development course for fifteen years, I would often look at the participants and think, "How come I see how fabulous they are, yet so many of them don't know it?" It was so difficult giving people evidence about their awesomeness yet watching them look at me with doubt.

Sometimes they would say, "You are the instructor; you are just saying that" and the answer was "No! I am really seeing who you really are! Why is it that you don't see it?" It was a true transformation when they got to see a glimpse of what I saw.

Become the person who sees through people to the gold inside. Be the person who knows, regardless of what people say and do, there is gold, there is love, there is good in their center.

When I struggle, I must stop myself to ask, is this struggle real or is it just a story? Is the story at the "gold" level or the "clay" level? You will find when you do this that most of our struggles are at the human "clay" level.

Being Right

> *"When given the choice between being right*
> *and being kind, choose kind."*
> —Dr. Wayne Dyer

Needing to always be right leads to pain and suffering. The very funny show from the 1970s *All in The Family,* was so successful because, although we laughed at Archie Bunker, we could also identify with him. His beliefs about people and about life were distorted, yet he expected everyone else to agree with his distorted views. He always had to be right. As we laughed, and through all the "dingbat" and "meathead" comments, we could also see how naive he was. Yet his wife, Edith, who came across as naive because of her loving nature toward all people, was often the voice of reason and wisdom in the show. She expressed her views lovingly and was often more clearly heard than Archie was.

Some people choose being right over everything else in life. We must put this in perspective. Is being right more important than being happy? Is being right more important than being abundant? Is being right more important than our loved ones? So many people are so attached to their beliefs that they are willing to lose everything in order to be right. People die over right or wrong. Yet since our ego and beliefs are distorted, our views on right and wrong are also often distorted.

Over the years of traveling around the world on business, I found myself traveling to Singapore. When a plane is about to land in Singapore, the flight attendants come around and ask that you dispose of any gum that you may have on you. Chewing gum is illegal in Singapore. Selling gum in Singapore can get one a jail sentence of two years. Possession of drugs in Singapore, such as 1,200 grams of opium, or 500 grams of cannabis, carries a mandatory death sentence. Punishment for lesser amounts is anywhere between canings to a life in prison sentence.

On my next trip to the Netherlands, as my colleagues and I explored Amsterdam, we saw the city turn around four p.m. During the day, the city seemed leisurely, and we visited museums, Anne Frank's house, and Van Gogh's house. But something happened at four p.m. The city became high-energy as the over one hundred and fifty coffee shops began to fill with customers. At the coffee shops you may buy coffee, but you also may buy any kind of "soft drug." You are even given a menu with the drug of the day.

So what is right? Who is right? We find that what is punishable by jail time, caning, or even a death sentence in one country may be totally legal and allowable in another. I embrace every culture and respect their conclusions on right and wrong. But I also question my beliefs and what is important to fight for and what is important to let go.

As I seem to be surrounded at times by people who must be right in everything they say, I only find few things in everyday life that I must be right about. Proving others wrong, victimizing others, making them feel defeated over unimportant things should be avoided. If you come from the perspective of compassion for others, you will find that many of the things you are right about may seem less important.

Take a step back on your position and determine if it is worth losing a friend or a relationship over being right. I often wonder how many arguments, fights, and wars would have been avoided if we didn't embrace our ego's need to be right. Our ability to influence someone is not achieved through winning an argument, a dispute, or even a war. Winning an argument may feel like a victory, but we've actually lost. Arguing never has positive results. Even if you win an argument, you will not be able to recover from others' resentment easily.

Avoid arguments; avoid the need to be right. You can state your opinion, but if someone disagrees with it, let it go. The only way they will see your point of view anyway will be if they trust you, respect you, and view you as their friend. Arguing and imposing your point of view on others will never achieve these things.

President Abraham Lincoln fought for great causes. However, when he had something bad to say to someone, he would write them a letter, then he would place it in his drawer. When he died, the letters were found, unsent. The greatest story on this is toward the end of the Civil War, President Lincoln ordered General Mead to capture Lee's army. General Mead procrastinated, and Lee and his army escaped. President Lincoln was furious. He wrote a letter to Mead but never sent it. He never said anything to General Mead, just encouraged him.

Lincoln is considered one of the greatest leaders because he respected people, freed people, yet he never openly showed anger or imposed his position on others. President Lincoln had learned how to use self-control, humility, compassion, and understanding. He knew that getting wrapped up in who was right and who was wrong is pointless.

Have the wisdom to see that winning in relationships is about compassion and understanding. Winning an argument or winning over someone brings about a temporary false feeling of satisfaction, followed by loss. When we push back on people or force them to admit they were wrong so we can see ourselves as right, it drives others toward justifying their actions, defending themselves, and ultimately, resenting you. (This is explained further in the Law of Action section of What You Resist Persists.)

Judgment

Much of our pain in relationships and in life is due to judgments. We think only our way is the right way. That makes everyone else wrong who doesn't agree with us. You see, this is how the ego works. Our ego is judging every situation as good or bad, everything as right or wrong; it very much separates us into friends or enemies. Judgment is the quickest way to despair. If we understand the importance of our differences, and when we understand that we are all one, then we will be less apt to harshly judge others.

Even if we are called to change the world for the better, we will be heard if we come from a place of love, rather than from a place of condemnation and judgment. We are living at a time of great change. I am seeing a world of acceptance, of love, of peace in the future. And all the change that will get us there seems to be happening right now.

We can make great change by visualizing the future state of the world and peacefully moving toward it. If you look at all the great people who brought about change and movement in the world, you will find people with a clear vision of the future moving everyone toward it with love and peace.

This is another area that is deceiving. Many believe that their freedom to choose is achieved through harsh judgment of the status quo. Actually, the judgment of the status quo without a clear vision of the future is what keeps us in the status quo.

This goes beyond judging others and judging situations in our world and our lives. It also applies to judging ourselves. We are our own worst judge sometimes. Give yourself a break. Know the goodness and the gold within you. Live in a positive mindset. Live your purpose, live an intentional life. You can spend lots of time judging yourself badly, or you can spend the same time creating a clear vision of your future. (More to come on the Vision and Purpose of Life chapter.)

If we are looking to achieve true freedom, give up judgment and view things as "just is." And if I must judge it, then I judge it as "all good." This does not mean that I don't have a vision that will make everything better. And this doesn't mean that the Universe doesn't have even greater things in store for you far beyond your vision. My friend Linda often interrupts me to remind me that it's not "all good." But we always agree that it just is.

We should not try to live up to others' judgments, but at the same time, we should not expect others to live up to our standards. We should give each person the permission to be the fabulous person they are, give ourselves the permission to be the fabulous people we are, and we should surround ourselves with people who do not expect us to be someone other than ourselves.

Judging ourselves brings about most of the drama in life. Most reality shows are based on characters that receive and, in exchange, express judgment. It is entertaining, but this drama does not lead you to a happy, peaceful life. What if something terrible has happened to us or to our loved ones? How could we not judge it? Then we need healing and time. Much of the content of this book should support us in the healing process and help us get through it and to the other side.

Action

Since we are the judge and the jury of our life, let's judge everything in a positive way. Let's assume that everything is as it should be. It takes faith to believe things are bad. What if we applied that faith into believing all is exactly as it should be? And what if our life is filled with things we really don't want? Then we can concentrate on our vision of the future, which we will be discussing in the upcoming chapters.

The Man with a Horse

In China I heard a story that is so inspirational, I always share it in my courses. Once there was a man who had a horse. All his neighbors came to remind him how lucky he was to be a farmer with a horse. The man said, "I don't know."

One day the horse ran away. All his neighbors came again to tell him how unlucky he was. Now he would have to do everything without a horse. The man said, "I don't know."

The horse went out and found friends and came back with four untamed horses. All the neighbors came again to say how lucky he was now that he had five horses. The man said, "I don't know."

When the farmer's son tried to tame one of the horses, he fell off the horse and broke his leg. Again the neighbors came to tell him how terrible it was that the son broke his leg. Now there was no one else to help him. The man said, "I don't know."

A war broke out in the country, and they came to the village to recruit all men to go to a battle they were expected to lose. Every young man went except the farmer's son, because he had a broken leg. The neighbors came to say how lucky he was that the son didn't have to go to battle. The farmer said, "I don't know."

The story goes on for another 400 verses. The moral of the story is to never judge your life. If you look at your life, it is a series of what people may consider good then bad. But actually, it is not good, and it is not bad. It just is. It is your fabulous, one-of-a-kind life. If you must judge it, consider that it is all good. If you are going through a breakdown, a tsunami right now, please look up and see the rainbow in the sky. If you don't look, you will miss the rainbow, the miracle, the view of your greatness waiting for you just on the other side.

Inspire others, encourage them, trust them. Write your angry letters, write your "I am right" letters without sending, openly publishing, or expressing them. If someone hurts my feelings, I use the Love Letter by John Gray in *Men Are from Mars, Women Are from Venus*:

The Letters Exercise

Below is the template I use for the Love Letters I write to all. It doesn't matter if it is a man or a woman, this is my "go to" letter when I find myself with hurt feelings:

1. You write the letter to them using the below beginning phrases:

    Dear _____,

    I am angry because _____

    I am sad because _____

I fear _____

I regret _____

Love,

(Your name)

2. You then write yourself a letter with the message that you would like to receive from them in reply to your letter (in step 1).

You will be surprised as to how good you feel reading the answer you wish the person would provide you. Even though you wrote the reply yourself, there is a fulfillment that you feel in having what you always wanted to hear. In this process, you also realize how difficult it is for someone else to know what you want to hear, just like it is difficult for us to know what others would love to hear from us. When we apologize, we are always guessing as to whether it will be accepted by the other person and whether we are doing it in accordance to what they are expecting. This is a very rewarding exercise.

Feeling Compassion

My father lived in the United States for thirty years, yet he could not learn to speak English. He was able to read and write English perfectly. It was just the speech and oral understanding of the language that he couldn't master. Yet when he passed away in the US, there were over 250 people at his funeral. There were people who didn't speak Greek that told me that he was their best friend. He had a state police escort since his best friend's son was in the state police at the time. As he was driven to the cemetery, people stopped because it seemed like someone important had died. Yet my father was a carpenter from Greece who did not speak English. How was this achieved?

Every Saturday morning, my father, who didn't know anything about cars, would go to our cars in the street and open a hood. He was not sure what he was looking at, but he looked at the engine for several hours. Sometimes he would check if there was oil in the car. He would clean and shine the engine.

As he was outside, people would approach him and would start talking to him. He never said to anyone, "I don't speak English." He would shake their hand; he would smile and say, "Hello," and he would let them talk.

When he came into the house, my mother and I would ask him how he carried on a conversation with them. He never knew what they said to him, but he always answered with how they felt. He was not sure of the content of the conversation, but he would say "something good happened, I think he bought a new car" or "I felt his sadness, someone must be sick in his family." "He is having problems with his family," he would say and sigh. "I wish I knew how to help." He felt their happiness, sorrow, pain, even though he did not understand the words and the details.

If you approached the conversation, you would see that he would shake his head "yes" as though he understood what the speaker was describing, and he would even periodically say

"Yes," as he allowed the other person to carry on. Sometimes he would say "No!" as though whatever they were saying was shocking to him. He would smile, shake their hand goodbye, and look into the speaker's eyes.

This went on for years. It was with sadness that I had to tell people crying at his funeral that my father did not speak English. They would insist he did. They felt understood by him. They felt listened to by him. They felt important, and they felt respected. Talking to my father had become part of their weekly routine. And although he may not have understood their words, he did connect with them and understand their struggles and their pain. He was able to give them a smile. He was able to make them feel important because he was happy to see them come by every week.

I often wondered if he did that with me. When I was growing up, my father worked in a furniture factory next to my house. I would go to talk to him while he was working. I remember going on and on about everything that happened in school, and he would say very little. But what he did say, turned out to be words of deep wisdom now that I understand it. When I complained about what others had done to me, he would hear my point of view, and then he would ask me to describe to him the same story from the other person's perspective. He wanted me to understand both sides.

I don't know if he listened to the details, but it was almost predictable as to what he would say. And for some reason, I still went to talk to him, and I still went through the exercise of presenting the issue from the other person's point of view. Somehow it gave me a deeper understanding of the situation. It also helped me release it.

I learned from my father that it really doesn't take much to give others what fulfills them. Everyone needs respect. Everyone needs someone to hear them. Everyone needs to feel important, have someone look at them lovingly, smile at them, accept them, and make them feel like everything is all right. My father was able to give compassion without even speaking the language. It should be so much easier for us. It takes patience. It takes liking yourself, caring for others, and it takes compassion.

Listening with Our Heart

Genuinely listening to others requires being interested in other people. Even if others are talking to us, we will not hear them if we are totally not interested in them. One of the reasons that many of us have difficulty remembering names is because we don't take that extra time to hear the name and associate it with this beautiful person who is just as important as we are.

In teaching personal development courses, I find that I am able to remember people's names so much easier in the classes than I do in the outside world. As people share their stories, I get to associate their name with their story, their pain, their happiness. The minute I feel what they say, it seems that this is when there is a connection, a "click" where now we are one. And, of course I remember them, not only temporarily, but for years to come.

There are some key things to know about people. Just like we have needs, so do they. They want to be loved, just like we do. They want to feel important, just like we do. They like to know that someone cares for them, just like we do. Our ego tells us that we are separate from others. It encourages us to judge others as different beings we don't understand. It encourages us to compare ourselves to others, to create a ranking of who is important and who is not. It is so important to know that in reality we are more the same than we are different. It is so important to listen to one another and to acknowledge what we hear and what we see in our heart after hearing them. I have witnessed people arguing so many times when, if they listened to what each other was saying, they would find they are in full agreement with one another.

Throughout our lives we take communication courses, writing courses, presentation courses; we are taught to read, write, speak. When was the last time we took a course in listening, feeling, or expressing compassion? For most of us it is never. Yet if we study successful people, we will find that emotional intelligence more strongly contributes to success than any of the other measures we have in place. IQ and grades are secondary to emotional intelligence.

It is very rare anymore that we come across a good listener. There are many reasons for this. One reason is distractions. On any given moment I find myself on a conference call while looking at email, while getting texts and instant messages. Somehow I believe I am listening and paying attention to it all, but as you know, it is unlikely. Other times when we hear the other person's point of view, we can't wait to jump in and express our view. Most communication is views being thrown at each other.

Yet acknowledging others, repeating back what you think you heard from them, is so very gratifying. When you hear someone speak, ask yourself, "What does this tell me about this person?" Many times you think you hear one thing, and when you repeat back you realize that you have added your filters and attachments onto it. It is indeed a great exchange when we listen, play back, acknowledge that we not only heard what the other person had to say, but also what they meant. Then we can express our view.

Let's make it a practice to listen to others, even if we don't agree with what they are saying. Many people stop listening or try to express their point of view when they disagree with what the other person is saying. Let's be the person that is open to hearing all views. Very often my friends tell me about shows they watch on TV and how they change the channel when someone is saying something they don't agree with. To me it is enlightening to listen to all views.

At a minimum, listening to opposing views gives us the opportunity to understand where others are coming from. If you really listen, you will understand what values are important to them. These may be values that are just as important to you. Sometimes these values may not be as important to you. The bottom line is that you will better understand. Understanding, acknowledging, waiting to be asked before expressing our opinion are enlightening steps in our growth. Let's acknowledge that we heard them. Let's repeat back what we think we heard. Let's make others feel heard and important; then it is more likely they will hear our views.

Others' Perspectives

Everyone seems to have a perspective on everything. We can listen to others' perspectives. We must remember it is their life, their filter, their reality. This is extra difficult for us as parents. Although something is not real for us, others' views, including our adult children's, must be respected as their truth. It is the same with our perspective. Our perspective is not good or bad; it just is. It is very freeing to not feel obligated to agree or disagree with others.

Letting go of trying to get others to agree with you is the most freeing thing you can do. Allowing others to experience life the way they need to experience it is the most loving thing you can do. We must remember that everyone has his own journey in life. We have our journey, and we must be respectful of others' journeys. We can share our story, and it should be okay if others don't understand it or don't want to follow it.

During the self-development classes I taught, there were exercises where people had to defend the opposite position of how they felt about key social issues. The process was first to understand that your position is not really "you." It is just a thought, a belief. Once you can detach yourself from your beliefs, then you can see things from the other person's point of view.

Again, keep in mind that the other person's point of view has also gone through filtering. If we respect others enough to allow them to have their own beliefs and thoughts, and if we understand that this has nothing to do with us, we achieve yet another freedom. We can become neutral about what others say, especially to us or about us.

It is freeing to not take anything that anyone else says personally. Every person spends the majority of their day thinking about themselves. Thinking that others' actions have anything to do with us only brings us pain. It is most likely not true, and it has nothing to do with us. We must remember that what others think of us is none of our business. What we think of others is none of their business. It is so very important that who we are is not affected by what others say or do.

We must decide who we are. Your "I am" list may include: "I am a person of integrity; I am honest; I am a good friend; I am a good parent; I am a good neighbor; I am generous; I am a caring person." Who you are should not change based on what others do. Good will attract good; negative will attract negative. If you consistently create good, have good things to say, or do good things, you will attract good into your life. As Judge Judy says, "When you do good things, good things happen. And when you do bad things, bad things happen."

Never allow others to control who you are. Regardless of whether someone is nice to you or not nice to you, your response should be based on who you are, not your reaction toward them. When someone is not nice, the best thing we can do is send them blessings. If you feel you need to protect yourself from them, then you must distance yourself.

I live in a neighborhood that has a lot of drama. I watch people react to each other, and often see people's character depend on what other people do. This brings us down to a very primitive vibration--the vibration that triggers fights, war, and constant drama and pain. Be who you are regardless of how others act around you. Then you will find yourself immune to the drama and all the negativity that is taking place around you.

What do we do if someone criticizes us or says things about us? We have a choice of taking it personally or understanding that it most likely has nothing to do with us. If someone says something good about us, we can say, "Thank you," as this is more a reflection about them than it is about us. And if someone says anything negative about us, we can again put things in perspective.

Since most people only think about themselves, imagine what a great compliment it is when they spend any time thinking or talking about us at all! Not reacting to others is a noble skill. Imagine how many arguments, how many fights, how many battles would be averted if one of the persons in the argument had the wisdom to not respond or to step away.

When we feel offended and feel we must seek revenge, we actually take our power and give it to the other person. When you decide to live an intentional life, and not a life that is based on others, you become untouchable. Your future will be filled with all you wish for and more, and if others try to bring you down it becomes irrelevant because they can't. Decide to be a person who lives an intentional life. Most people's lives are a series of reactions based on how others treat them. We don't realize that reacting gives our power away to others.

Ideas to Ponder

- In dealing with others, we must be forgiving, kind, honest, and happy despite how others react. It is not between us and others; it is between us and God.

- Guard your character and hold on to your values regardless of how others behave. Be the person who is always loving, kind, and don't give your power away just because someone who behaves badly enters your journey. Be you regardless of what others may say or do to you.

- Regardless of how others act, we should look to see the gold in their center. Everyone has gold in their core. Connect with others at the true self level. Don't be fooled by the clay.

- Every person is looking to feel understood and important. Be compassionate and look to understand where others are coming from.

- Connect with others with your heart. Remember there are no language and ego limitations when you connect at the heart level.

- Judging yourself, things, and others allows your ego to take over and create havoc in your life. Accept things as they are, without judgment, and find gratefulness for everything in your life.

- Allow your children to experience their journey. Don't impose your ways on them, unless they ask.

Chapter 6

Looking for Others' Approval

When we are constantly looking for others' approval, things get chaotic. I have several examples even today where I find myself looking for others' approval, and I also have several examples where I have overcome this need. When we are looking for the approval of others, eventually it will become an overwhelming and painful experience. This is because when we are at this level of neediness for approval, we are operating at a level far away from our true self. We lose our freedom and become a slave to others' reactions and judgments of us.

It becomes especially painful when it has to do with the approval of important people in our lives: our family, our close friends, people we truly care about. People can approve of us one minute and disapprove of us the next. When we are looking for others' approval, an alarm should ring loudly in our mind. It is an alarm that highlights the danger ahead and tells us we have some inner work to do.

It is normally during times when things get shaky in my life that I realize and become aware that I must connect with my true self in order to live with happiness and freedom. How do I know things are back to normal again? When the love within overflows from me to the world, when I am living based on my terms and not based on what other people think or say.

Comedy

During a short period of my life, I entered the world of comedy (I will be discussing this more in the chapter regarding Synchronicity.). I got to perform with the most amazing comedians—my famous teachers and not-so-famous fellow comedy travelers. It seemed the greatest struggle comedians have is handling the occasional disapproval from the audience.

In every comedian's life, there are good nights and bad nights. How the crowd will react is unpredictable. I viewed comedy as a mental exercise in disregarding the approval (or non-approval) of others. I would tell myself every time I went out to perform, there would be people who loved my act and people who would not like, or even hate, my act.

In every audience there will be at least one person who is not thrilled about the performance. Although most performers focus on the ones who don't like what they see, I saw comedy as an exercise of having so much fun, it didn't matter. I focused on the people who laughed, who seemed to have a good time and liked what they saw, instead of those who didn't react or even heckled.

It was a true privilege when my fellow comedians used to say, "Do we have Maria perform first to make the crowd feel good, or do we have her go last so the crowd leaves feeling good?" The secret was to have fun, regardless, and to convey the love within, even when talking about and making fun of not very nice things that happened in our lives. This is actually the secret in everything we do. If you are doing your best, if you are having fun, and if you do not get wrapped up in other people's (and your own) garbage, you will find yourself peaceful, joyful, and happy.

How do you deal with other people's stuff? Just know that most of the time it is not even about you. Everyone is so wrapped up in themselves that they are not even thinking about you. If we have the wisdom to know this, we will know that whatever people say and whatever people do, is not about us. It is about them. We can then put things in perspective. It is something private. If we have something good to say, share it. If we don't like someone, or if we have something to say that we know will hurt others, then we must remind ourselves of our filter and skewed view.

When Others Don't Approve

If you are in the midst of a situation where you are being put down or getting hurt emotionally or physically, the first step is to recognize that through the years you have fallen out of like with yourself. You must get back to a space where you know that no one has the right to touch you or hurt you. No one is more important than you are.

You are everything good. You are beautiful, talented, abundant, brilliant, successful, courageous, decisive, complete, happy, open, worthy, adored, confident, genuine, giving, sensitive. And your potential is without limit! Your potential is greater than the ocean, greater than this planet. Don't believe the stories that hold you back. Imagine your potential and multiply it by a billion! We can never imagine the vastness of good things that is ahead of us.

A pine cone could never imagine itself as a beautiful pine tree or a forest. Yet that's what it becomes. A caterpillar could never imagine itself as the most beautiful, colorful butterfly. But that does not interfere with its ability to become it. Our purpose in life is to grow beyond our limitations, to become the best possible versions of ourselves. Yet unknowingly we stop our growth and transformation because of limited thoughts and beliefs that are not even true.

You must remember that most of the things others do or say have nothing to do with you. Most people spend the majority of their lives thinking and worrying about themselves. Although what other people do may seem personal, most of the times it is not. It is just people being careless and insensitive to others. Sometimes this comes from people you trust and never expect to be hurt by. Acknowledge the hurt and know that it is not about you.

Regarding Our Children

Sometimes the ones who don't approve are our children. As we live our own journey and we learn our lessons, sometimes the very hard way, we don't want our children to experience the same struggles we did. Out of love, we want to step in and impose our lessons on others, especially our children. Yet the ultimate expression of love is allowing others to live their journey. It is not our job to prevent contradictions in others' lives, but it is an expression of love to be there for them during times of happiness and sadness (without saying "I told you so.").

In discussing this with other parents, I received quite a pushback. Why wouldn't someone want advice from another person who has experienced life longer and may know what to do in certain situations? Wouldn't the advice from parents be classified as "education"? Why do adult children often not want to hear from their parents?

It is difficult to admit that perhaps our children want advice from other people. Sometimes our children go through phases of life where they become our critics. They have perceived our life based on their filter, and they have made decisions regarding things they may want to emulate in their lives and things they may not want to emulate.

Even though they may not want advice from us, they often do seek advice from others. It comes from people they trust or people whose lives they admire. It doesn't mean they don't love us; it means they are in a different journey than our journey. As loving parents, we can be happy that our children are looking to live their lives on their terms. The worst thing we can do is take this personally. We just need to be there for them if they ask for our wisdom and love them regardless.

Dishonesty

Dishonesty from others may run in your life like an endless loop. People who promise things they don't mean, people who present themselves as someone other than who they really are, people who try to challenge your integrity and character. For me it felt like the white noise running constantly in my life, making me feel vulnerable and unsure about what is real and what is fake. As I share in this book, you will run into dishonesty from needy people, and you will react based on what you know at the time.

It is easy to generalize and decide to not trust anyone, yet that would be a mistake. Just remember that this is not their purpose. You may have people in your life who are dishonest right now. If you have believed them and have made decisions in your life that you have come to regret, you will grow and learn from the encounter. The next time you are bound to approach relationships with more wisdom and knowledge. Try to look at things realistically and not generalize. It all becomes a lesson in your spiritual growth and freedom, a lesson in taking care of yourself and knowing the symptoms the next time you encounter them. You also learn to know when to forgive and when to distance yourself from anyone who could hurt you.

It is extremely important that you find the wisdom to never take things personally and to know there is a greater journey and a grander life purpose. We must also learn to walk away, in a loving and compassionate way, from things that can pull us downward. It is these people that you shouldn't allow in your life anymore, but this has to happen without resentment or drama. People that are self-centered with their neediness and drama will only hold you back from reaching your purpose in your journey to greatness.

Surround yourself with people who know their true self and exude love, compassion, and true friendship, people who will contribute to your growth and will not derail your growth. Do not hold grudges, because the person who did something that hurt you may not be the same person anymore. People change, just as you do. Give people the room they need to learn from their experiences and change. Our ego separates; our true self unites. It is true that some people may never change but give them the benefit of the doubt.

"You see, in the final analysis, it is between you and your God; It was never between you and them anyway."
—*Mother Teresa*

Words of Wisdom from My Father about Marriage

My father would say some funny things that may bring you a smile. He truly believed that the people that you are supposed to meet in your life you will meet without having to search for them. He did not let me date as a teenager, and I got quite upset, thinking I would never meet anyone and have a family. He always told me that the person I would marry would find me, even if I never went out of the house. This sounded ridiculous to me.

Well, one day the man that became my husband called me. He told me he was friends with my cousin in Greece (he was in New York), and asked if it was all right to come over to visit. I tried to convince my father that this was just a fluke, but my father smiled and said it was not a fluke. This was how it worked.

His theory on selecting a wife or a husband was also entertaining. My father claimed that selecting someone for marriage was like shopping for shoes. He claimed that most people have trouble with their marriage (and their feet) because they always select the pretty shoes rather than the comfortable shoes. Even if shoes don't fit perfectly, even if they hurt in certain spots, we still buy them because they are pretty. When my marriage didn't work out, again he said, "You picked the pretty shoes, didn't you?" Well, of course I had.

Whose Mess Is This Anyway?

Once other people enter our lives, it is easy to look at traumatic events and start blaming others for these events. This brings up every negative emotion. And negative emotions, unless you stop them, grow exponentially. This also makes us victims of other people. It makes us feel weak and often trapped.

Until a few years ago, I blamed my mother for pretty much everything. When I first met my ex-husband, she really liked him, and not only was she kind to him, she was so happy he had entered my life. When I met him, he was a college student, alone in the US, not speaking English very well, trying to go to school and make ends meet by working hard and figuring out how to pay for his tuition.

Once he became more independent, he started treating my mom with less and less respect. And when this was combined with her thinking that he was treating me badly, she didn't like him anymore. She was very comfortable in telling him what he did wrong, and he was very comfortable ignoring her, or worse yet, disrespecting her.

Until a few years ago, I partially blamed my mother for him leaving and for my divorce. The rest of the blame for the marriage not working out, I placed on him. And, of course, I had a long list of other things that my mother had done and he had done. When I felt alone, when I was facing overwhelming issues, I would get angrier and angrier at my mother and him. I felt like a victim.

So many of us blame our parents for our issues. It is so easy to blame others for our mess. After all, in every mess there is someone else who was a participant. Although it feels great when we repeat our stories of all the bad things others did to us, believing we are victims and sharing our stories of what others did to us actually keeps us in chains and brings more of that into our lives. It also gives us an excuse to be unkind to the people that we think caused bad things to happen in our lives.

Taking responsibility does not mean feeling guilty for things that happen in our life. Feelings of guilt, regret, and anger weaken us as people, lower our vibration, and, depending on how long we stay in a negative state, weaken us and derail us from our purposeful journey. Taking responsibility allows us to move forward with clear direction and intention. You can be the judge of you and everyone around you, or you can understand that your reaction to everything that happened in your life will create your outcome. You can choose to know that you are the victor of your life.

Why do we feel victimized? You will notice that most of our problems are problems as long as they are bigger than we are emotionally. What if we became stronger and bigger than our problem? Then our problem would be small and insignificant. Maybe our focus can be on how to grow bigger emotionally and spiritually. You are doing this by reading this book. The next chapter will give you more tools that will support your journey and transformation to your greatness. Talking about our problems and the drama just brings more problems and more drama into our lives. One of the ways to become bigger than everything that is going on in our lives is to take responsibility for it all. It is counterintuitive, yet it is one of the greatest things we can do for ourselves.

There are teachings that claim that before we enter the human world we get to choose our parents. There are also teachings that believe we choose all the participants in our life. These teachings suggest that we participated in the planning of our greatness. The bottom line is that we get to a place where we take full responsibility for our life, and we don't blame anyone. This is the freeing part about all this. If we are responsible for bringing things into our lives, then that means we can change them if we don't like them.

Please note that *responsible* doesn't mean that we should beat ourselves up for having things happen in our lives that we do not desire. When things happen, I am always intrigued and ask myself, "What am I supposed to learn from this?" It is great being surrounded with great friends who understand these concepts. Everyone and everything that enters our lives enters for a reason. Sometimes the reason is obvious, as it normally repeats itself. Other times it becomes clear as time goes by. If we take responsibility for everything in our life, and if something enters it that is undesirable, we are able to focus on practices and tools that will allow us to change it.

Ideas to Ponder

- Don't allow others' judgments to affect your spiritual growth. Don't give your power away to others.

- Have fun in all you do. Life will bring you great things beyond your imagination.

- In relationships, look for genuine people that treat you well and make you happy. Don't be dazzled by drama. Just like shoes, select relationships that are comfortable. The flashy shoes always hurt your feet, and relationships that are superficial will always hurt your heart.

- Always take responsibility for your life. Remember that how you react to things determines your outcomes.

PART 2

Chapter 7

Universal Laws and Practices

Religion or Spirituality?

I am often asked, "Are you religious?" I translate the question to mean, "Do you believe in a God or a group of gods and following the rules and practices of an organized religion?" This is an awkward question, especially when asked by someone who is spiritual. The answer is "Yes, I am religious."

I am also asked, "Are you spiritual?" I translate this question to mean, "Are you seeking to better understand your inner life? Do you believe in a higher power we call Spirit? Do you embrace compassion, empathy, and open-heartedness?" This is an awkward question, especially when asked by religious friends. The answer is, "Yes, I am spiritual."

I spend time with spiritual people of all religions and no religions. As spiritual people, we, too, forget that looking down on religious people is just ego separating us. In my opinion, if you are a religious person or if you are a spiritual person, what you have in common is looking to expand your soul, become one with the Universe, Spirit, or your God. Although every spiritual practice approaches that goal differently, and although every religion has its unique way of achieving this, the goal is the same.

We all feel that our spiritual practice or our religion is the best. And this is great, as every spiritual practice and every religion has its spiritual beauty. No person can dictate any other person's spiritual journey, and it is almost dangerous to isolate someone within a religious box or a spiritual box.

If you are an exclusively spiritual person, you will often find that religion played a huge part in your journey to becoming a spiritual person. Any criticisms you may have accumulated against traditional religions led you to being a spiritual person. Therefore, religion played a role in getting you to where you are.

If you are exclusively a religious person, may I ask you to consider that perhaps this is not the only way a person finds God? Everyone's journey is different.

My personal answer to the question of religious versus spiritual is, "I am very spiritually religious." To translate, I am very spiritual, which I couldn't achieve without being very religious. And I could have never become very religious without understanding spirituality. My religion allows me to understand spirituality. Within my religion I was taught of a God who is *agape* (pure love). I have met so many people I have considered great spiritual teachers in my religion: Father Aloupis, Father Constantelos, and many more.

I have also met amazing spiritual teachers outside of my religion, like Wayne Dyer and Louise Hay, and many others in the spiritual community, who still live on. My religion has taught me about spirituality, and spirituality has explained things about my religion that are often not discussed.

I often find myself right in the middle of things with many questions. Once I went to teach Sunday school at a nearby church (not in the church where I grew up). The judgment and criticism from my original church was overwhelming. I didn't want to leave my original church; everyone there is like my family. I love everyone there so very much but found myself distancing from the negative energy. This was how I learned how dangerous judgments can be. I was going to another church but the same religion. Others will not understand that you must follow your heart and your spiritual journey, but you must.

On a business trip to China, I found myself missing going to church. I asked one of my coworkers whether it was alright for her to take me with her to temple. On a Sunday morning I stood at a beautiful Buddhist temple. Outside there was (what I called) holy water that everyone was partaking in. It reminded me of my church. We have holy water too. I walked into the temple that was filled with incense and smelled just like my church. Everyone prayed, and so did I. You see, they prayed to their gods, I prayed to Jesus and my God. I felt uplifted and connected with everyone else in the temple, as we all experienced connection with our higher beings.

In the question of spiritual or religious, I find that the right answer is only yours. It is your journey to greatness that you need to follow. My journey is being a devout Greek Orthodox Christian at more than one church, who embraces spiritual practices that enter my life experience. I pray and meditate with everyone and anywhere, as the goal is to awaken to our oneness with Spirit, with God. Awaken to our purpose, awaken to the journey toward becoming the best version of us that we are meant to become, awaken to knowing that happiness and joy come as we find ourselves in that path of transformation, soul expansion, connection to our true self and our personal greatness. Will life be easy? Will life be hard? The answer lies within our reaction to our experiences.

God, Source, Spirit, Universe

Regardless of the name we use for God, most religions say that we believe in a being that has created the universe, that is unconditional Love, that is Life. This being is all-knowing, eternal, and ever-present in the universe at all times. God is life. Without God, life ceases to exist.

Whether spiritual or religious, I see a very close correlation in the description of God. In spirituality I have heard God described as Spirit, Body, Soul. In Christian religions, God is Father, Son, Holy Spirit. So what we know about God both from a religious perspective and spiritual perspective is that there is a Mind of God, a Spirit of God, and a Son or a Body of God.

One Sunday morning, I was leading a discussion about God with the most beautiful group of teenagers. The discussion was around understanding God from a religious perspective, and if we are made in the image of God, then how to understand ourselves within that context. Being made in his image seems to be a topic somewhat confusing for people. I have heard several people argue over what "made in his image" means. Some people understand this in physical terms and wonder what God looks like. Some argue whether God is male or female. Some argue over skin color. Yet whether spiritual or religious, we can simply say that having God's image means that we, too, have a mind, a body, and a spirit.

As we are human, we understand the physical, the body version of ourselves. When it comes to our mind, many understand our conscious mind. However, the subconscious mind, as described in the Law of Correspondence and the Law of Attraction later in this chapter, creates our physical experience. Our subconscious mind holds our beliefs, which are also energy, and eventually manifests these beliefs in the physical realm. Sometimes even though we are not aware of some of our beliefs, they may unconsciously direct our actions and ultimately our life experience.

The Universal mind from a spiritual perspective, or the Father from a religious perspective, has the power to create. The Father/Universal Mind creates in conjunction with the Spirit through thought, word, vibrational energy, and attraction. Spiritually and religiously the Spirit of God is associated with the enablement of Universal Law. Many Christian religions agree, as the Holy Spirit is seen as the enactor of miracles, transforming the physical into the mystical. We pray that the Holy Spirit is always with us, and we yearn for miracles in our lives. Although most people see the physical, religion, and spirituality as three separate concepts, totally separate, I see them totally connected.

Science or Spirituality?

One of the ways that we seem to separate ourselves is by science versus spirituality. It is assumed that there are two sides. One that supports data and logic, the other that supports emotion and faith. Yet in 1687, Isaac Newton wrote, "This most beautiful system of the sun, planets and comets, could only proceed from the counsel and dominion of an intelligent and powerful being." I agree with Isaac Newton, so I am very interested any time science makes a discovery that brings science and spirituality closer together. I know that science will prove the existence of God; it is just a matter of time.

It was very exciting for me to see in 2013 Francois Englert and Peter Higgs win the Nobel Prize in Physics for their theory on how particles acquire mass. Peter Higgs had been working on this theory since the 1960s. Prior to Englert and Higgs, physics explained how particles and forces interact with one another but did not explain how particles get their mass or how mass was originated.

The theory explained that a subatomic particle must exist that is the building block of the universe. This particle was called the "Higgs boson" and the "God particle." The God particle is not a religious term, it is a scientific term to describe a field that is everywhere, in all spaces. Particles attract the God particle which interacts with them and creates mass. This God particle is believed to be the origin of mass.

It was also very exciting for me when with the discovery of the quantum physics microscope and the study of nanoscopic layers, the existing of a moving energy in the center of all things was confirmed. Many, including me, had seen this ever-present moving energy as the proof of the ever-presence of God.

One morning at a function, I was elated to be introduced to one of the men who worked on the quantum physics microscope in Switzerland. I had so many questions. "What did you see? Was it amazing to be a scientist who can prove the existence of God?"

He looked at me quite puzzled. He smiled as he told me how surprised the scientists were that so many people thought this moving energy was God. He candidly stated that to him and his fellow scientists, this is not God, it is just moving energy at the center of all things.

Is it God? I look forward to the day when science, religion, and spirituality emerge. Scientists like Bryan Enderle in his TEDx talk "Science vs. God" are making great strides. I know that it is only a matter of time.

Ideas to Ponder

- God is unconditional love, creator, eternal life.

- God, Source, Universe is Spirit, Body, Soul (or Father, Son, Holy Spirit).

- We are made in the image of God as we, too, have a mind, body, spirit.

- We create ceaselessly, as we are constantly creating thoughts.

- We have a conscious and subconscious mind. Although we know what we are thinking in our conscious mind, very often there are beliefs in our subconscious mind that we are not aware of.

- Our subconscious mind creates our reality through our thoughts, beliefs, and vibration.

- Father/Mind creates through thoughts, word, vibrational energy; Spirit enables non-physical to physical and creates miracles.

- Through the quantum microscope, energy is seen at the center of all things.

Chapter 8

Universal Laws

Understanding basic Universal Laws provides insight into understanding ourselves, our life, the world, and the Universe.

1. The Law of Spiritual Oneness

Our ego leads us to believe that each of us is separate, that we are all independent beings. The Law of Spiritual Oneness confirms that Spirit is in everything and connects everything. We are all one. The plants, animals, planets, people—we are all connected. Everything we do affects everything and everyone in the Universe.

In the Greek Orthodox religion, in our Sunday services the priest bows to the Spirit within each person. When holy communion is offered, we are called to receive "the holy gifts for the holy people of God." There is holiness in every person through God's Spirit. There is holiness in every living thing. It is the "gold" referenced in the Clay Buddha story.

As humans we think we are more important than every other living thing. However, just like we take care of ourselves, we must take care of our earth and all living things. This is very hard to do, especially when those around us don't understand this Universal Law.

2. Law of Vibration

We are all energy. Everything in the Universe is energy. Everything emits a vibrational frequency at all times. When we hear loud music, we can feel the vibration. We know that our voice has a vibration. The Greek philosopher Pythagoras used to prescribe music as medicine because vibrational frequency impacts us at the cellular level. (I especially enjoy listening to music at the Love frequency of 528 hz!) This law plays a huge part in what we attract throughout our day, since our thoughts and feelings emit vibrational frequencies. See table in The Feeling Filter chapter.

3. Law of Correspondence

The Law of Correspondence acknowledges that our outer world is only a reflection of our inner world. This may be confusing, because at the conscious level we can look at our life and know that it is not the way we want it to be. Our outer world reflects our subconscious mind. This is where all our beliefs and thoughts are stored. Most of our thoughts pass unnoticed. Most of our beliefs are buried in our subconscious mind. As all the Universal Laws work together, we do have the capability to change any belief at the conscious level, and through repetition embed it into our subconscious level. Our vision and affirmations practice is a way to override beliefs that do not serve us and replace them with beliefs we desire in our lives.

4. Law of Cause and Effect

Every religion acknowledges this law. Every action we take has an effect. In some religions it's called karma. In the Bible we read of actions and consequences. In the Christian religions, the New Testament of the Bible becomes our guide on how to live our lives in order to have good consequences. The Apostle Paul stated, "You reap what you sow." Although every religion is different, if you look at it from a very high level, positive actions based on love have positive consequences, and negative actions, intentions, thoughts produce negative results. Love is the overarching way to living a life with positive consequences.

5. Law of Compensation

This Universal Law acknowledges that all our deeds are compensated. Although this law is normally associated with a monetary or physical compensation, we can view this law as all the compensation we receive in life, all the blessings we are grateful for. As we give to others, we will receive. We should be happy to give to others, always coming from a place of generosity, and let this law take care of itself.

6. Law of Perpetual Transmutation of Energy

This Universal Law states that energy is perpetually changing form. The most familiar example referenced with this law is the transmutation of water. Water is H_2O which, when vibrating more slowly, changes to ice, and when vibrating faster changes to steam. This law defines energy as a form that cannot be created or destroyed. Non-physical energy turns into physical energy, and physical energy changes into non-physical. A thought is an energy wave which, when repeated, becomes a belief in our subconscious mind. A belief in our subconscious mind, per the Law of Attraction, can transform into the physical. Everything has energy within it, as proven in quantum physics and as seen through quantum microscopes.

7. Law of Relativity

The Law of Relativity states that something becomes real when it is related to something else. Experiencing a pandemic gives you a better appreciation of health and well-being. A long lockdown causes you to appreciate freedom to go anywhere you want. Worrying about well-being teaches you to appreciate feeling secure. Experiencing darkness gives us an appreciation of light.

As we experience life, the Law of Relativity also helps us to keep things in perspective. When we are going through a personal challenge, sometimes we think that what we are going through is the worst possible situation that anyone has ever experienced. This law teaches us that whatever our situation, it is always in relationship to other similar situations. There is always someone else who is going through something better, and someone who is going through something more serious. This law teaches us to keep our challenges in proper perspective and to stay as positive as we can.

Another reference to the Law of Relativity is the comparison of our spiritual growth to the size of our problems. Sometimes our problem seems big because we feel small in relation to the problem. As we spiritually grow and evolve, as we move toward our greatness, problems that seemed big before will seem insignificant.

8. Law of Opposites (Polarity)

The Law of Opposites states that within everything lies its opposite. This is also called polarity or contradiction. This is what allows us to fully experience and appreciate the good in our life.

Understanding Contradictions

Many times when we think one of the Universal Laws does not work, it is because we don't understand the Law of Opposites. When it comes to what we judge as "bad" things in our lives, could they just be the Law of Opposites at work? Is this what is needed in order for us to appreciate the next part of our journey?

Even when you look at the Adam and Eve story, you can see that without having experienced contradiction, they could never imagine what "after the fruit" would be like. They had nothing to compare their life against. I had been asked so many times throughout the years why Adam and Eve selected the fruit from the tree of knowledge. I had given the normal answers of "They were tricked by the snake," "They didn't obey God," and so on.

Now I realize that if we don't have contradiction in our lives, we don't have the ability to understand or even imagine the consequences of having the opposite of what we are experiencing. In the case of Adam and Eve, how could they ever imagine the human experience when all they had experienced was the joy of living in the light and embrace of God? It is contradiction that gives our life intelligent choice. We can ask, "Why would they ever choose this?" That's because coming from a human perspective, we can see the before and after. At that point in time, they can only see the before. With lack of contradiction, they did not know what separation meant. There may have been curiosity, but most likely they never expected the "after" experience.

When something "bad" is happening in the world, I always know that it may just be a contradiction and that the opposite will follow. When good follows, there is such a vast appreciation of that good because we have experienced the opposite.

As I am writing this book, we are still in the midst of the Coronavirus pandemic. Everyone's life has been impacted by this pandemic, and everyone is trying to understand why this is happening. What I am noticing is that an unfulfilled wish we all have is a world of peace, love, a place where everyone only wants good things for their neighbor, regardless of what country, race, religion, or any other thing that has traditionally separated us.

Peace, love, health, oneness are intuitively states that our true self embraces and things that we crave as human beings. Is it possible that the pandemic is a contradiction? Is it the something that is happening that is other than what we want, that will be followed by exactly what we asked for?

There are several things that happened during this pandemic. One of the things that I found myself, my family, and my friends doing is praying. We all seemed to pray, not only for each other, but for everyone's well-being. I received so many calls from friends and acquaintances asking me if I needed help. I called neighbors and friends to see if they needed anything and asked how I could help them. Everyone was ready to help anyone who needed support.

During the pandemic there were some other horrific things that happened that heightened our awareness of racism. Again, the opposite happened of what is in our heart, which is the reality that all lives are important, we should all treat each other with respect and value each other, the reality that we are all one. I look forward to having all that is happening bring us to a place of wisdom and truth.

Could all that is happening be the vehicle through which after this is all over, everyone's vibration will be elevated with the wisdom of knowing that we are all one? Could this be the vehicle through which we will embrace each other and create the world that we always wished for? The world of peace and love, a place of joy where we are all one.

By understanding the Law of Opposites, could we anticipate that people will develop an appreciation of health, an appreciation of being together with others, an appreciation of celebrations, an increased level of compassion and love for others, and a global understanding of how every human being on this planet is connected with one another? Could all this have a negative effect? Could this contradiction create future fear and worry about viruses and germs, and a fear of freely being with others?

From one perspective, contradictions trigger great lessons. On the other hand, they may trigger fear-based filters for people who don't understand this law. I welcome the gratitude that this contradiction, the pandemic, will cause. We will all need to become aware of our filters so that we are able to put the fear it may generate into perspective.

As stated in the Fear and Negative Thinking chapter, we confront fear by understanding that most of the time it is false and by drowning it in gratefulness and faith.

9. Law of Gender

The Law of Gender confirms balance in the Universe. In all aspects of creation, you will find masculine and feminine. Creation does not occur without this balance. We see this in all planes, the physical, mental, and spiritual. In order for something to be created and grow, it needs both masculine and feminine forces. In Taoism there is Yin and Yang. In spirituality, there is the heavenly and earthly, the soul and the ego. In many Christian faiths, Jesus represents the masculine energy, while the Virgin Mary represents the compassionate, nurturing, feminine energy. Both genders exist in everyone.

There needs to be a balance between our actions and our compassion, our mind and our heart.

10. Law of Attraction

Like frequencies and vibrations attract like. This law works closely with all the Universal Laws, and especially with the Law of Vibration. As we vibrate at certain frequencies, we attract into our lives people and experiences at the same frequency. As there is vibrational energy and frequency, so is there attraction. We create our experiences.

About a year ago, I moved into a new position at work. As I was about to fly to the UK for my company's sales conference, I decided as a gift to myself, and for the trip, to purchase an expensive designer handbag. It was absolutely beautiful! It was black with the designer initials engraved across the front of the bag in black. The handles were made of leather, and there were beautiful gold chains on each of the two handles.

The bag did not fully close on top, but I didn't think it would be a problem since it had a magnet that closed the center of the bag. I believed that the magnet was so strong, that it was bound to close, regardless of how full the bag was. Given all the mishaps that followed with the bag, it highlighted that whoever designed this did not understand the concept of magnets!

In everyday use, this magnet caught on everything that went by it, which prevented its proper closure. The bag would fall in the car, and when I would try to pick it up by its handles, the chains on the handles would snap onto the magnet making it impossible to pick the bag up. When you looked at the magnet, you would see every conceivable thing attached to it, except the closure. The closure of my wallet would get attached to the magnet, and my wallet would eventually fall out of the bag. I had a metal ring on my cell phone. The ring would get attached to the magnet, causing me to decide to never put my cell phone in my handbag ever again. Things attached to the magnet would eventually fall out of the bag while walking in the street, up the stairs, everywhere.

Then I realized that this is exactly what happens to all of us! We do not understand the magnet in our lives called the Law of Attraction. As we let our thoughts and feelings run rampant, we many times attract into our lives the opposite of all we desire.

The Law of Attraction was very simply explained in elementary terms in the video and book *The Secret*. At an oversimplified level, the Law of Attraction is activated by an Ask, further fueled by Belief, and finally delivered when we are ready to Receive it. Within this oversimplified explanation, there are other elements in action not fully stressed in the video and book. First, there are basic Universal Laws such as:

1. There is only Love.
2. There is only Positive.
3. There is only the Present.
4. You are energy, and your vibration is transmitted into the Universe every moment.

Ask

This is something we do constantly. I am convinced that every thought we have is an Ask. Throughout our day we observe our environment, and we respond to life with positive and negative thoughts depending on how we translate what is going on through our filter. Our thoughts trigger emotions which also fuel our Ask. Once I asked the participants of one of my workshops, "What if every thought is a Prayer? Or what if every thought is an Ask?" I actually saw people cringe! Becoming aware of our thoughts, and especially our vibrational energy, is extremely important. Also, deciding to attract intentionally rather than reactively plays a huge role in this area.

There is only Love

In our Ask we must be very careful and aware of Universal Laws. What if there is only love in our Universe? What happens when our emotions are away from love? If we pay attention, we may see the Universe just translates the negative emotion to love. The reason I say this is that so many times I hear people talk about all the things they hate. They hate their house, their car, their clothes, their nose, their body, their job, their boss; the list can go on and on. And it seems that the more people complain the more they become stuck in that situation.

What if the Universe turns the word *hate*, as an example, to *love*. I hate my house gets translated into I love my house. Therefore, the Universe responds by attracting "staying there." So perhaps in order to create something new, we must be at peace with the old. Thinking, "I love my car and would love a bigger one" would attract a bigger car. "I love my house and would love one with a driveway" would attract the driveway.

This is why in my many years in business, I have seen so many people quit their jobs because they hate them. Yet when they get a new job, the exact same circumstances continue to appear, and sometimes are more accentuated than previously.

In cases where we are in unacceptable conditions, and it is very difficult to make peace with them, we can use the power of vision and affirmations to change our future.

There is only Positive

When I work with my clients to create a vision, I find that people can more easily describe what they no longer want rather than describe what they do want. They will say, "I don't want to be in debt anymore" rather than say "I want to be abundant." "I don't want a job where I have to work long hours," rather than say "I want work-life balance."

Mother Theresa understood this concept well. Once someone asked Mother Theresa to join an anti-war rally. She answered, "Invite me when you have a rally for peace." What if all the "anti" movements actually attract prolongation of whatever they are fighting against? It is important that in our lives we support solutions (positive) rather than fighting problems (negative).

There is only the Present

We must know that whatever happened in the past, however great or heinous, there is nothing we can do to change it. We should definitely learn from our past, yet it is very important that we do not get stuck there. So many people are stuck in situations of the past. Yet life continues to move forward, and it moves fast. It is like driving a car forward at seventy miles an hour with a blocked windshield and using only the rearview mirror. The car will crash.

Being stuck in the past, while life is racing forward, creates more of the past. The greatest part of being human is that every moment is an opportunity to redirect our future. It is in the present that we create what is to come. Make sure that your thoughts in the present create the future you desire.

Believe

The reason I refer to the inner voice throughout this book is that it plays such a huge part in the Law of Attraction. For example, what if we were to practice the Law of Attraction and decide to ask the Universe for one million dollars? The level at which we believe that this is possible plays a huge part in whether we will receive the one million dollars or not. Our inner voice very often overrides thoughts and actions and prevents our upward vibrational spiral. If you begin expecting one million dollars to enter your life, but your inner voice tells you there is no way this is possible, this unbelief will block it from coming to you.

My way of dealing with this is to acknowledge what the inner voice tells me and to respond to it in several steps. One, is by welcoming it. Anything we push away, will come back with even more force. What you resist, persists. We must welcome this inner voice that is actually a thought trying to protect us. This is the voice that during primitive times kept people in the cave to prevent them from being eaten by wild animals.

Two, I thank my inner voice for protecting me and trying to prevent me from getting hurt. "Welcome, and thank you for being there and for protecting me. I agree with you that having a million dollars can be overwhelming, new, and dangerous, but that was only yesterday, today all is safe." You will see your inner voice quiet down and disappear. Then you release it. You must embrace your inner voice in order to have the ability to let it go. Throughout this book I provide you with more tools to override your inner voice and begin believing that what you are asking for is possible.

Other beliefs may also block the one million dollars coming to you. For example, a belief that millionaires are people who take advantage of others, or a belief that they are selfish or those who put money above people and relationships, could prevent the manifestation of one million dollars. We must be mindful of our thoughts and beliefs. We must be happy and positive toward others who have what we desire. Having negative feelings toward others who have the things we want tells the Universe that is not something we really desire. We must remember that this is a loving, positive Universe.

Receive

This is the third aspect of the Law of Attraction. In order to receive what we ask for, we must be ready to receive it.

The aspect of Ask, Believe, and Receive came especially to light as I read the Bible. In the New Testament, I noticed how often after Jesus performed a miracle he would say "Your faith has made you well." Our deep belief and faith that something will happen creates miracles. In these cases, people felt if they were in the presence of Jesus, they would become well.

In one case, as a crowd of people were around Jesus, a woman who had a bleeding issue touched him and immediately was healed. Jesus stopped and asked, "Who touched me?" as he felt the release of healing energy. He told the woman, "Your faith has made you well." As people expected to be healed in his presence, they received what they expected.

Personal Experience with the Law of Attraction

When the video and book *The Secret* first came out, I became very in tune with the Law of Attraction. I remember reading the book while I was in France on a business trip. I started thinking "dog" as a test. Well, very soon I realized that was not a very smart test because so many people in Versailles seemed to have small dogs you see in the street. Everywhere I looked, I saw small dogs. I immediately thought of this as a happenstance but didn't give up. I still kept thinking "dog."

One day my coworker came to pick me up so we could drive together to the office in Paris. As she was driving, she was cut off by a very small car. In the back seat was a huge, absolutely beautiful sheep dog. For miles, all we could see was the dog. My coworker kept commenting as to how unusual it was for someone to have such a big dog, and especially a big dog in a small car in France. Again, this may have been just happenstance, but I thought it may have been the Law of Attraction and me not giving up of the "dog" thought. This was a minor attraction. There were two major attractions that followed.

My friend and I worked at the same company. She was at director level; I was senior manager level. After several years of no bonuses, our company decided to give out bonuses. I was so happy about receiving a $20,000 bonus, until my friend shared that she was receiving $55,000. I understood she was a director and directors received higher bonuses than I did, but I decided I too wanted a $55,000 bonus. I wrote an affirmation that read, "I am now happy and grateful in receiving a $55,000 check from my company in addition to my salary." Well, this became my mantra for several months. I was totally shocked when my manager called to tell me my whole department was going to be out of a job. It took me a long time to accept this as true, because I just knew that this company was supposed to give me a bonus of $55,000. I accepted that I needed to find another job, and I was hired by my current company. Months later I received a check in the mail from my previous employer. My jaw dropped as it was a check for $55,000! The bottom line is, you will receive what you asked for, but not always the way you expected.

One night my ex-fiancé and I were watching *The Apprentice*. The job of the teams was to put together a marketing plan for a new car that Pontiac was designing called Solstice. I fell in love with that car. My ex-fiancé went to the dealer the following week, only to find that the car was not being manufactured yet and there was a high demand due to the show. As a result, the dealer indicated that when the car became available, it would most likely be sold above sticker price due to the demand.

After seeing the car, it was obvious this car did not fit my lifestyle. I worked during the day and taught courses in the evening. For the courses I needed to bring a lot of things to the meeting rooms that were normally in large hotels. A small, two-seater car would not be practical for the work and lifestyle I had.

Three years after my fiancé and I separated, I was with someone else. Without knowing anything about my love for this car, he saw it in an ad and decided this car was "me." I went to visit the dealer, and there it was ready for me! He insisted this car was meant for me. I have been driving the Solstice for ten years now, and every time it brings so much joy to know the Ask that I put out into the Universe became a reality, in its own time. It reminds me we do attract what we want into our lives, and only when we believe, and when we are ready to receive them, do they "appear" into our lives.

When the Law of Attraction Doesn't Work

There are several reasons the Ask you send out into the Universe may not come about as you planned. These are prerequisites in order to make your Ask more effective:

1. Love what you have as you Ask for what you want. The Universe doesn't translate the negative well.

2. Create your affirmations and vision in present tense. "I am now happy and grateful that ___". Express happy emotion, feel the joy in having what you desire.

3. Truly believe it is possible. Know anything is possible.

4. Be aware of your thoughts and be aware of your vibration.

5. If the opposite of what you asked for appears, it means the process is working. You are going through a contradiction before what you desire arrives.

If you are not mindful of your thoughts and the vibration you emanate, you become just like the magnet on my handbag. You attract anything and everything except what you want to attract in your life. You become the magnet of your thoughts. Positive attracts positive, and sadly, negative thoughts make you a magnet for negative things.

In engaging the Law of Attraction, a big part in allowing it to work is staying in the energy of joy, love, abundance, gratefulness. Many of my friends make blanket statements of how the Law of Attraction does not work. I tell you, my dear friends, it does… always. But what you must be aware of is that the Universe has very creative ways of giving you what you wish for.

11. Law of Rhythm

When we use the Law of Attraction, we normally expect things to appear in our lives immediately. However, the Law of Rhythm tells us that the Universe has a rhythm. The vibration described in the Law of Vibration works within Universal rhythms. Many describe this like a pendulum that goes back and forth. Within this rhythm there is a divine order, and everything we desire will come to us at the right time.

People who do not understand the Law of Rhythm will sometimes conclude that other laws, such as the Law of Attraction, do not work. Everything comes at the right time, within the Universal Law of Rhythm. Finding the rhythm of whatever we are trying to achieve becomes extremely important. Imagine trying to surf if you cannot become one with the rhythm of the waves. Imagine trying to sing if you cannot find the rhythm of the music. In the Law of Attraction, becoming one with the rhythm of what we desire is necessary in order to manifest what we wish to attract in our life.

12. Law of Action

There are several aspects of the Law of Action that we need to understand. From one perspective, things are not as simple as Ask, Believe, Receive in the Law of Attraction. There are some practices that are necessary in order for our intentions (non-physical) to manifest in the physical. These practices are described below. As we begin our practices, we will notice things happening in our life. We must take action to open the doors of opportunity that may be coming in our lives. We must have faith in the process, and take action to move things forward.

What You Resist Persists

Another important aspect that we must understand is that the Law of Action correlates to Newton's Third Law which states that if one object exerts force on another object, the second object will exert equal force in the opposite direction to the first object. In a simplistic term, we cannot push without expecting a push back. If the forces are pretty much equal, we may even have a situation that persists for a long time.

This second aspect of the Law of Action is the reality of "what you resist persists." It is so important to understand what we try to resist or get out of our lives will most likely persist until we approach it from an acceptance and positive perspective. As explained in the Law of Attraction section, we must begin accepting and embracing what is, in order to be able to change it. Resisting only keeps what is in place indefinitely.

Ideas to Ponder

1. We are all one (Law of Spiritual Oneness).

2. Everything is energy and vibration (Law of Vibration).

3. Our outer world is a reflection of our inner world—or subconscious mind (Law of Correspondence).

4. Every cause has an effect—you reap what you sow" (Law of Cause and Effect).

5. We are compensated for our actions. Even if we try to only give, we still receive joy and fulfillment (Law of Compensation).

6. Energy is perpetually changing form. It cannot be created or destroyed. Energy changes from non-physical to physical, and from physical to non-physical (Law of Perpetual Transmutation of Energy).

7. Everything is relative. Challenging situations get us to appreciate all good things that follow (Law of Relativity).

8. Within everything lies its opposite. Understanding this concept gives tsunamis and all difficulties a different perspective. Knowing that a contradiction triggers growth needed for appreciation of the opposite (which is what we desire), makes us understand that even difficult situations are moving us toward positive results (Law of Opposites).

9. Both masculine and female forces are needed. Action and compassion, mind and heart are both needed in order for creation and growth (Law of Gender).

10. The Law of Attraction works with other Universal Laws to attract everything into our experience.

11. The Law of Rhythm assures that all we attract come to us when we achieve the rhythm and vibration of the item we desire.

12. The Law of Action requires us to take action as experiences enter into our lives in order to move toward our desires and our greatness.

What we resist persists. In order to bring about change be "for" causes. Being "anti" creates persistence.

Chapter 9

Life Purpose, Vision, and Affirmations

When you build any physical structure, you begin with the foundation. The foundation of your life is your Purpose. All of us have a life purpose. So many of us progress through life without knowing or understanding what our purpose is. It is important to take the time to determine what your life purpose is. This takes some introspection. When you know the purpose of your life, it becomes easier to create your visions and affirmations. The Universal Laws, along with the Law of Attraction, will bring into your experience the things you desire.

Life Purpose

So many of my memories as a child and as an adult involve loving being in the spotlight and feeling unique. I was an only child, so I had my parents' full attention and then some. I have clear memories that go back to when I was two and three years old. Back then, I loved to sing. That did not stop with singing at home. When my parents would take me on a bus or a train, I would start singing. When we would go to visit friends and family, again, more opportunities to sing. And people would clap and talk about how I made their ride nicer. As I grew older, I would recite poems. My parents started entering me in talent competitions, and I would win, not necessarily because of talent, but mainly because of personality.

I remember being entered in a contest when I was four years old. My father spent hours practicing a poem with me that I was supposed to recite in the competition. It was called, "The Four Seasons." He indicated in the entry that I was going to recite a poem. When it was my turn, the MC announced my name, and that I was going to recite a poem. When he gave me the microphone, I announced that I was going to sing a song. It was a very funny Greek song about a guy being forced in marriage ("Ela Vre Haralambi"). The audience was laughing, and clapping, and since I got the most audience reaction, I won.

When we came to the US, I was the first child in that elementary school that was from another country and didn't speak English. The spotlight followed me in college when I was on the Greek radio program, "The Voice of Greece." Many of my after-work activities have involved teaching and leading the youth at my church for over thirty years, teaching a popular self-development/professional development course for fifteen years, being involved with Toastmasters, doing comedy for many years, teaching Jack Canfield's *Success Principles* workshops, teaching workshops at Toastmasters conferences, the list goes on and on. When giving an inspiring speech or workshop, I feel the joy of being on purpose. It feels like I become a new person; that's when I come to life. If I am coaching, if I am mentoring, if I am inspiring others' personal, emotional, or spiritual growth, I am on purpose.

Although I knew in the back of my mind that this was my purpose, my life changed when my friend Linda gave me a unique birthday gift. She created for me my Human Design chart. The chart highlighted that my centers are all defined, which provides me with a clear purpose and direction. People with defined centers radiate energy out into the world. People with undefined centers are attracted to people with defined centers. Although I always suspected that I had more clarity than others around me, this provided me the confirmation that this is what was actually happening in my life.

Knowing your life purpose makes you passionate about doing what you are here to do. You find yourself loving what you do and feeling the joy of being on purpose. I have come across people who believe they do not have a life purpose. Everyone has a life purpose! It is a matter of remembering. It starts by thinking back on your life and remembering your unique gifts and talents. Then write down the times you remember when you have used these gifts and have felt pure joy, knowing that this is what you are meant to do in life.

One of my friends insisted that she has never felt joy in her life. If that is true for you, I would recommend getting a Human Design chart done, or alternatively take the *Passion Test* by Janet and Chris Attwood. Jack Canfield's *Success Principles* also provides a template through which you can define your life purpose easily. Knowing your purpose is the foundation for creating your vision and goals and feeling the passion that comes from living an intentional life. But if you are convinced that there is nothing you are passionate about, or you do not have one particular thing that you feel joyful about, then you just might be a hummingbird.

Might You Be A Hummingbird?

I was humbled to hear a talk by Elizabeth Gilbert, the author of *"Eat, Pray, Love."* She received a letter from someone in her audience who had done everything possible to find her life purpose, but she just could not find it. When people asked her to define her passion, to define her joy, just like my friend, she was not able to define it.

Elizabeth Gilbert realized that there are brilliant people in her life that don't operate with a sense of purpose and passion. Telling you to find your purpose could create anxiety, tension, and a feeling of exclusion, a sense of something being wrong if you cannot find your one purpose. Elizabeth eloquently in her speech separates people into Jackhammers and Hummingbirds. Some people just know what their purpose is, and they become the jackhammers toward that passion. If you do not know what your purpose is, there is nothing wrong, you might just be a hummingbird. The hummingbird goes from flower to flower, from tree to tree, and as it does that, it cross-pollinates the world.

If you cannot find your purpose, Elizabeth proposes that you turn your head one-quarter inch either way, and then just follow your curiosity. Look at the clues, follow them. They may lead to something, or they may lead to nothing. Then look for the next clue, and the next. Live a curiosity-driven life. One day you will realize that these clues led you to exactly where you are supposed to be. Your curiosity may lead you to your purpose and your passion. There is a sacredness in every place that you are in your life. And always know that you are perfect.

Vision and Affirmations

Our mind allows us to travel beyond our reality. When someone tells us a story or when we watch a movie or a show, we find ourselves transported into that experience through the power of our mind. In our mind's eye we can go to our favorite vacation spot right now. We have a choice of where we want to spend our time and we can choose positive thoughts to take us to very fabulous places. Unfortunately, many people choose negative thoughts which transport them to very horrific places.

Mark Twain said, "I've lived through some terrible things in my life, some of which actually happened." Sometimes in our mind's eye we take ourselves to some terrible places. Our subconscious mind does not know the difference between thought and reality. It assumes that if we are thinking it, then it must be true, so it brings it to us. Many sports teams use visualization as a way of attracting their desired outcome (to win). If we know that our mind works this way, why not change the movie we are thinking from a horror movie to a beautiful adventure filled with all our wishes come true?

When Disney World was opening its doors in Orlando, Florida, one reporter told Mrs. Disney that it was very unfortunate Walt had passed away and never got to see it. With total confidence, Mrs. Disney looked at the reporter and said, "He had seen it, in every detail." When interviewed after the opening of EPCOT, Mrs. Disney said, "But the thing that is so wonderful is because he had this vision before he died, it's been carried on so completely. That's what would make him feel so good. When we would go out to eat, he'd take a paper napkin [makes motion of drawing on it] and tell me 'We're going to do this, and we're going to do that and have all these countries come in and all' and it's happened, which I think is wonderful." Walt Disney had clearly seen all his parks even when they were drawings on a napkin. That's how strong our vision is. Many times when my vision came true, it seemed like it was not a big deal because it had become a reality in my subconscious long before it came about. Therefore, when it actually happened, it seemed like it was inevitable or "old news."

In creating the vision for your life, you can choose the type of vision you want to create. You can start with a Life Vision, a Long-Term Vision (two to ten years from now), and a Short-Term Vision. Alternatively, you can have multiple short-term visions that are consistent with your life purpose or your purpose of ultimate curiosity. In creating a Life Vision, think of how you would like to be remembered by others. After we transition, how would we want our friends to remember us?

My friend Dennis has a Life Vision comprised of two words, "He cares." This is how he wants the world to remember him. This vision totally describes him. Dennis is always there when someone needs any kind of help or support.

One day as I was passing a coworker in the hallway at work, I turned to say "Hello" to him, and as he said, "Hello" he put his palm on his chest and fell backward to the floor.

My instinct was to run away, and the great thing was that I was able to run to Dennis who ran to the man on the floor, fell down on his knees, held the man's hand, and started talking to him as though everything was normal. While Dennis was tending to our coworker, I called 911 and our medical department for help.

Dennis said to the man with a smile, "Well this is a fine way to try to get out of work." Even though the man was in distress, I watched him smile back as Dennis assured him we were right there for him, and he was going to be all right.

A few minutes later the company nurse came, and only a few minutes after that the ambulance came. The man had a mild heart attack but recovered beautifully. I learned that day that perhaps it was a good thing I never entered the medical field, but I was so grateful for Dennis and people like him.

Dennis is always Santa Claus at Christmas. He also volunteers for Christian Overcomers, particularly at the summer camps where he fully takes care of the handicapped and disabled. His Life Vision of "He cares" still drives his long-term and short-term goals.

Exercise: Take a few minutes and write or draw your Life Vision, Long-Term Vision, and Short-Term Vision.

It is fun to picture your visions as though they are a movie you are watching. As an example, if you are looking to get promoted in two months from now, you can express your vision by describing what a day two months from now would be like. If you are looking to lose weight, describe a day as it would play out with your new weight. If you are looking to be in a new relationship, describe how it would play out as if it is happening right now.

As an example, "It is March 1. I am so happy and grateful as I wake up, get on the scale, and I am 120 pounds. I put on my pants, and they seemed so loose at the waist. I go to work and am so grateful as everyone comments how great I look. I am leaving work on time today because I am making sure I work out before it gets dark."

If you do not use the present tense but reference some future timeframe, as an example, "I am going to lose weight in two months" the Universe will respond with you are always going to lose weight in two months (which will never come).

Affirmations are a great tool to bring our focus and attention to a desired future or outcome. Affirmations also play a big role in overriding unwanted beliefs with desired beliefs. Our reality always reflects the thoughts and beliefs of our subconscious mind. Within our subconscious mind there are beliefs we may not even be aware of that are controlling our current reality. Our vision and our affirmations create a new focus for our subconscious mind.

Many times our vision and our affirmations are questioned by our subconscious mind through our inner voice. If you picture yourself in your vision and your affirmations with one million dollars, but your reality is not so, as you repeat your vision and affirmations, you may hear some internal pushback. This is the reason earlier on in the book we addressed our inner voice. Any pushback must be addressed immediately. One way of quieting the voice is to reply that whatever the voice is telling you was true yesterday, but from this point forward it will be different. If you are envisioning yourself with one million dollars and you hear your inner voice questioning you, respond with, "That was true yesterday, but from this point forward I am a millionaire."

Another important aspect of your vision is that you must make it positive. It is a positive Universe which seems to not hear the negative words. If your affirmation is "I am no longer in debt," it seems to translate it to "I am in debt." If your affirmation is "I am no longer sick," it seems to hear "I am sick." You must make your affirmations positive. "I am now happy and grateful that I am healthy."

Your affirmations may address all aspects of your life or specific aspects you desire to change. In my vision I address health and well-being, love and relationships, finance goals, career goals, lifestyle, hobbies, giving back to the world.

"I am now happy and grateful that I am 120 pounds by March 1.

"I am now happy and grateful that I am eating vegetables and fruits every day."

"I am now happy and grateful that my income is $____."

"I am now happy and grateful that my title is _____."

When you read your affirmations daily (but if you can, multiple times a day), you must feel them and be enthusiastic about having achieved them in order to evoke the Law of Attraction. Become enthusiastic as you envision your affirmations entering your life experience. The word enthusiasm comes from two Greek words. *En* (within) and *theos* (God). It is the God within you. With enthusiasm you can envision and cross human boundaries. Enthusiasm creates miracles in your life. It is also important that you read your affirmations every day for thirty days. It has been scientifically proven that it takes thirty days for your subconscious to accept your affirmations as reality.

Ideas to Ponder

- We all have a life purpose that is the foundation of our life. We may not realize what the purpose is until later in life. Be okay with being a hummingbird and follow your curiosity.

- Our vision and affirmations should be consistent with our life purpose as well as our Life Vision.

- Our goal is to live an intentional life. Most people in the world live a reactive life based on current circumstances.

- Think about your Life Vision and how you would like to be remembered.

- Create affirmations and afformations. Afformations are affirmations in the form of a question: "Why am I now happy and grateful that _____?"

- Write your affirmations in present forms and feel them as though they are happening now. "I will be" or "I am going to" should not be used. Using these phrases creates an experience where you always "will be" expecting your affirmations to happen or you are always "going to" be experiencing what you expect. Use phrases like "I am now happy and grateful that…"

- When reading your affirmations, express emotion of gratefulness, and read them with enthusiasm.

Chapter 10

Practices

Our Two Jobs

In describing the major practices that I follow, I will summarize how I view each day when I wake up. What I now understand is that life is pretty simple. We have two jobs in this life. One is to love ourselves and all others with all our heart. The second is to forgive ourselves and others with all our heart and soul.

This is easy to do if we approach things from love, our true self. This is difficult to do if we approach things from our human self. Although difficult sometimes from a human/ego perspective, it is important to love and forgive in order to achieve peace and happiness.

Wayne Dyer used to say hating others is like taking poison and expecting someone else to die. When we have negative feelings for others, it just eats us up. And as we express the negative feelings, the only thing others see is our behavior. We are expressing a dark side that most people just don't want to be around.

If we approach loving and forgiving others from our true self, it is much easier. Our true self is connected to God, so it only knows Love, Peace, Happiness, Abundance, Eternity, Joy. Our human self is filled with stories we perceive, assumptions we make. It is filled with hurt feelings, broken hearts, pain, struggle. It is filled with our ego. The only truth is our true self, and how we approach life is a choice. We can choose to approach things from a true-self perspective or from a human perspective. Once we think someone has hurt us, or once we think something has not turned out the way we expected, unless we release it right away, we create layers and layers of things that need to be scrubbed and released, which becomes a long, tedious process.

I use several methods of releasing. These methods both help release as well as raise the vibrational frequency for the day. Also, we must remember that every day gives us the opportunity to start anew. Every day is an infinitely abundant day filled with blessings. The past does not dictate the future; every morning gives us the opportunity to adjust our vibration, release the stories, and begin with pure love.

Morning Practices

My mornings are pretty busy as most days I must be on calls by seven a.m. I wake up one hour prior to the start of my business day, and I begin the morning with gratefulness. I take out my gratefulness journal and begin by writing a minimum of five things I am grateful for on this day.

Next, is *A Daily Dose of Love* by Christine Kloser. This starts my morning with gratefulness and inspiration every day.

If we can hold on to a positive, grateful thought for twenty seconds first thing in the morning, we will find that our whole day will have a positive trajectory.

This is followed by my religious prayers. Whatever religious or spiritual practice you follow, this is a good time to connect with God as you begin the day. As part of these prayers, I ask God for direction and ask to be guided in accordance with His will.

Next, I read my Vision followed by my affirmations and express happy emotion and enthusiasm that they have come about (in my mind). I visualize each affirmation and am so happy to be attracting each statement into my experience. Everything is connected. God's will, our Purpose, our visions, our affirmations, and our daily activities are all things that bring us joy and life fulfillment.

I then look at my calendar for the day, and I notice things I look forward to doing, things I dread doing, and things I will be doing that I am pretty much neutral about.

The Sedona Method (Sedona.com) helps me release things I look forward to and things I dread. This can be purchased from Sedona.com, Programs and Events, Programs, Other Programs, Beginning and End of Day Release ($24.97 at the time of writing this book). The module I purchased is called "The Beginning and End of the Day Release." The module includes a morning release and end of the day release, and a series of releases that help in dealing with people that may enter our day. I only use the beginning and end of day releases daily. I use the other releases occasionally.

Next is what I call my "Lists" meditation. I have created three lists. The first lists all the people in my life that I love (my wonderful family, my friends, coworkers). The second is people in my life that I feel I must forgive. The third is people in my life that I must ask for forgiveness. I look at each person on the list of people I love, and in my mind's eye, I feel them near me and as I feel so grateful for having them in my life, I send them love and blessings. I do the same with the second list, except to each of these people I also send forgiveness. For the people on the third list, I feel them with me, as I send them my sincere apology and ask for forgiveness. These lists include people who are still alive and people who have transitioned.

The last thing I do every morning (and this takes about five minutes) is Donna Eden's Daily Energy Routine. You can find Donna Eden's Energy routines on YouTube.

When I don't have time to do all my morning practices before I start the day, I do them throughout the morning. You can do the "Begin the Day" release any time, even while you are driving.

These practices help me start my day with purpose, intention, direction, and with a clean slate.

Midday Practices

There are three midday practices. On certain days I spend one hour and do them all together, on other days I split them throughout the day.

- **Ten minutes – Ho'oponopono**

Ho'oponopono is a Hawaiian release practice that is amazing. It is very simple because it is the repetition of the phrases "I am sorry," "Please forgive me," "I thank you," and "I love you." YouTube has several Ho'oponopono meditations. I use the song version that is about eight minutes.

"I am sorry" is associated with having attracted things in our lives as a result of beliefs in our subconscious. "Please forgive me" releases these beliefs and clears the slate for our future. "I thank you" is consistent with feeling gratefulness for our life and experiences. Having things in our life we don't expect gives us the opportunity to release them. We can feel gratefulness for the opportunity to release beliefs that do not serve us. "I love you" brings us home to the energy of love, the energy that we truly are. Ho'opnonopono activates miracles. I often do this release for others by looking at a picture as I chant the four miraculous statements.

- **Ten minutes – daily mantras**

One of the best investments you can make is Deva Premal and Miten's *21-Day Mantra Meditation Journey*. You can feel the difference in your life when you do these mantras every day consistently. Everything in your life will become calm and peaceful and a sense of joy will fill your heart.

- **Thirty minutes — Genpo Roshi Big Mind meditation**

For thirty minutes I sit as the "Non-seeking" and "Non-grasping" Mind, "Big Mind." During this meditation I repeat, "I am the

Non-seeking, Non-grasping Mind. I do not need to seek or grasp anything." Throughout the meditation, I notice my mind wander sometimes and try to seek or grasp. By reminding myself that I am sitting as the Non-seeking, Non-Grasping mind, thoughts begin to come up, but immediately bounce away. At the end of this meditation you will find yourself with a clear mind, feeling totally connected to Source. After this meditation I find myself coming up with many new, creative ideas. It is thirty minutes well spent in the middle of your day and clears your mind of all stresses from the morning.

Night Practice

Every night I read my vision statement and visualize the vision as if it is happening now. Next, are the affirmations. My affirmations are in two different formats in PowerPoint. I have one affirmation per slide. The first affirmation format is "I am now happy and grateful that…"

Another way to activate affirmations is by putting them in question form. The second format of my affirmations are in question form. These are called *afformations*. If you ask yourself "Why am I happy and grateful now that _____?" your subconscious mind assumes that this has already occurred, and it does all it can to bring what you ask into your experience. Some nights I use the affirmation format; most nights I use the afformations format.

The second nighttime practice is a religious practice. In my religion, we have a prayer called "The Jesus prayer." "Lord Jesus Christ, Son of God, Have Mercy on Me." This is a protection prayer. I use a prayer rope (*komposkini*) with this prayer. This is my religious practice; whatever religion you are, use your own religious practice. My Catholic friends use a Holy Rosary for their evening prayer practice. In the Deva Premal and Miten mantras there are two mantras specifically for protection; you may use these during your night practice if you prefer.

My third nighttime practice is a releasing practice. I fall asleep listening to the Sedona "End of Day" meditation. Through this meditation I release any upsets of the day, even ones that sometimes I didn't know I had. As Hale Dwoskin asks the questions, issues (positive and negative) that need to be released come up. It is great going to sleep feeling connected to God, feeling protected, and with a "clean slate."

Other Practices
Gratefulness – the Most Important Practice

Being grateful and acknowledging our appreciation is a learned, important habit. Genuine gratitude pushes out negative thoughts and replaces them with a pure emotion of fulfillment and joy. A child is always happy and acknowledges their happiness and gratefulness through a smile, a game, a hug. As we grow older, we begin taking things for granted. Since being grateful is not instinctive, it takes work.

We must remind ourselves to be grateful throughout our day. In my meeting with teenagers every week, I asked them to write five things that happened in the past week they were grateful about. The first week they were stunned.

They stared at me because they had a very difficult time coming up with two things. They complained that a week is a very short time frame. Nothing really happens in a week. So I told them I would share what I am grateful about from the last two hours.

I was grateful that I woke up, because I know many people didn't. I was grateful that I am blessed with my son, who is always there for me and brightens my life. I was grateful that even though it's wintertime, my home was warm. I was grateful for my comfortable bed, for my blankets, for my home. I was grateful for the blessings in my home and the food in the refrigerator, because I know there are many people in the world that have nothing to eat. I am grateful that I opened the closet and had to pause in deciding what to wear today, as many people do not have clothes. I am grateful that I am able to go out and that I can walk because only a few years earlier, before my hip surgery, walking was so very difficult; I had to walk with a cane, and I was in so much pain. I am grateful for all the beautiful faces in my group of teenagers that I am blessed to be with.

Immediately they began to write. We now start every gathering with this exercise. It is something that became easier as the weeks went by. Even in the Bible there is a story of Jesus healing ten lepers. One came back to thank him; nine took their miraculous healing for granted. Gratitude transforms us and brings us joy. When we are grateful, we are happy to give, to help, to be there for others.

Gratefulness Actions That Will Impact Our Lives

In interacting with others, let's come from a place of love with everyone we meet, even the more challenging people in our lives. Let's be genuinely grateful for them, and not only thank them, but tell them why we are thanking them. Just like you crave attention and importance, so do they. Instead of just saying "Thank you," add the reason. "Thank you for greeting me with a smile today; it is appreciated." "Thank you for your kindness today." "Thank you for listening, for caring, for being supportive, for making the day nicer, for..." You fill in the blank.

If you are feeling down, if you are feeling depressed, if you want to stop a panic in its tracks, start thinking (and writing if you can) about things you are grateful for in your life. Gratefulness will play a key role throughout your journey. Take a notebook and a pen, keep them together and declare them your gratefulness package.

For years I have been writing a minimum of five things I am grateful about each morning. Now I can't stop at five! I have pages of things I am grateful for every day. In the beginning you may have a difficult time coming up with five things. Do your best. I find myself being thankful for specific people in my life for being there as my friends, and even the ones that are there as the contradiction in my life.

I am often grateful for my washing machine, that I can do other things while washing clothes. I remember my grandmother washing clothes by hand outside and spending her whole day washing clothes. I am grateful for the weather. I am grateful for my son, and I am grateful every time we watch *Jeopardy* together (as he knows most answers, and I struggle) and laugh. I am thankful for everything and everyone that crosses my life every day. I am grateful for all who shine their light in my life. This practice actually shifts the energy of our life upward. Through gratefulness, our life can totally turn around and we can begin to see amazing change.

A word of caution. When it comes to others, do not expect others to be grateful back. Gratefulness is a learned attribute, and it seems that most people forget to appreciate what others do for them. If you expect gratefulness, you will most likely be disappointed. If you don't expect it and you receive it, it will mean so much more. Don't forget that whatever you do for others should not be out of need or in order to get something back; it should come from your heart.

Loving Everyone

In our natural human state, our tendency when we look at others is to look for differences. Thinking we are separate is an illusion. The Coronavirus pandemic has shown us how we are all one. Let's approach others with love in our hearts, and let's find all that we have in common. Let's look at each other with eyes of compassion and understanding.

Remember that all of us have the same core. One Spirit runs through us and connects us. Also remember the story of the Clay Buddha. Remember that what we see in others is deceiving. Most people have their "clay" on display. The gold is what we have in common.

Let's openly express our love to others, not because you need them and not because they need you, but because of who you are and who they are. We are love. When anything other than love, compassion, or support is expressed, the pain and struggle begin. We must always keep in mind that our ego separates, our "true self" unites. When you look at others negatively, just remember this is your ego only seeing the clay. If you approach others from your "true self" you will see their "gold." Seeing the gold in others and in ourselves allows us to see beyond what our eyes can see. We begin seeing with our heart and soul.

Forgiveness
Forgiving everyone

My father used to say, "Love your friends with all their faults." This has been a struggle throughout my life. Regardless of what anyone did to my father, he would forgive them. Now, my father took this to the extreme. Even people who hurt him, or took advantage of him, he would forgive, and he would allow them back into his life.

During my early years I used to see this as a weakness. I can now see that this was part of his greatness. He had evolved to the point where he would not allow things he considered trivial to affect him. Did people take advantage of him? The answer is yes, but it didn't matter. He had reached a level of wisdom where no one could actually hurt him. This may be true for you too. My goal is to someday evolve to my father's spiritual level. I must admit I am not there yet, but I know what it looks like, and I can see the road to that level clearly.

Forgiven but apart

Although we should look to love and forgive, unless we have reached a spiritual level where others' actions do not affect us or the level where we are attracting kind, loving people, we must protect ourselves and be selective about who we choose to have in our life. If anyone is hurting you physically or emotionally, you must protect yourself, you must distance yourself. You are not in this life to be a martyr or a doormat to others.

Loving people and forgiving people does not mean allowing people to hurt us. And it does not mean making excuses for people who may be abusive to us. So be mindful of yourself, and be mindful of others, and take care of you. You are in this life to thrive and shine and become the very best version of yourself you can be.

If your circumstance is such that you are truly getting hurt, where you are sustaining physical or emotional injuries that will be with you for a long time, then it is time to forgive, but distance yourself from people who hurt and abuse you.

Love and abusive relationships

There are so many times that bad things are happening in a relationship, but we continue to stay because we are so "in love." Don't let thoughts such as "I love her" or "I love him" keep you in abusive relationships. If someone is hurting you, it is not love.

I am not speaking with judgment here. I have stayed in relationships longer than I should have because of what I thought to be true love. If you step away from abusive relationships and focus on healing, you will see that it is the greatest gift you can give yourself. Any time you think you need something or someone, you will find yourself in a position of compromise. Do not compromise yourself, and most importantly, don't give your power away to people who are self-serving and do not treat you the way you should be treated. You deserve to be peaceful and happy.

Being in love in an abusive relationship is equivalent to addiction. What would happen if you were a recovering alcoholic? When you are an alcoholic and someone offers you a drink, you accept it, even when you know it is hurting you. If you are a recovering alcoholic, you would refuse the drink. This is how difficult walking away from an abusive relationship can be. Especially if you are convinced you are in love with your abuser. You need to tell yourself you are in recovery in order to break off the abuse and possibly save your life.

And you must be strong enough to resist when the abuser tells you that they love you and they are sorry they hurt you. Remember to love yourself and step away. This is not your person. Your person, the one that you are meant to spend the rest of your life with, will treat you with love and respect and will never think of hurting you. Tell yourself, "I am addicted to ____, and I am committed to get over this addiction."

When this person calls, writes, or shows up at your door, look at them as the addiction you must get over and get away. People show up because the more they show up the longer it will take you to get over them. Do all you can to stay away so you can heal and be on the road to the life you are supposed to live.

You will also find that once you are healed, you will attract healthy relationships into your life. Ending this relationship is not the end of the world, even though it feels that way. You deserve a good life. Just like getting over any addiction, it is not easy, but you must love yourself enough to give yourself the gift of good people and a good life.

Practices for Raising Your Vibrational Frequency

Knowing how to raise your vibrational frequency, how to reach and connect with your true self, becomes important in accessing your true self and receiving the experiences you desire. There are several practices to follow in raising your vibrational frequency. When we sleep, our vibrational frequency resets. It is important when we wake in the morning or after a nap, we adopt a practice that brings us joy and positivity. My morning routine I described in the Morning Practices chapter assures a good start to the day. Here are some additional ways to quickly raise your vibration.

- A quick way to raise your vibration is by listening to your favorite music.

- Do you love to dance? Then dance! When I am alone at home, I play my favorite music and dance.

- I also like to sing silly songs that make me happy. "Zippidy Doo Dah" can only bring a smile. "Shaboom" is another favorite. "I Love to Laugh" from *Mary Poppins* brings about a happy, joyous morning.

- Writing or doing anything creative (art, music, and so on) connects you with Spirit and raises your vibration.

- Read a favorite book that inspires you. *A Daily Dose of Love* by Christine Kloser is my favorite.

Find what inspires you and do it. It may be yoga or a walk in nature or around the block. The important thing is that you become aware of your vibration and joyfulness level. Do all you can to raise it by doing what you love doing.

Religious Practices

In addition to spiritual practices, there are many religious practices. An important Christian prayer is the Lord's Prayer. According to the Bible, this prayer was given to us by Jesus as a way to pray. Throughout my life it has brought me peace when I was afraid, and is one I use at any time.

In addition to the Lord's Prayer, my Greek Orthodox religion offers beautiful prayers and chants that elevate our vibration and connect us to God. "Kirie Eleison" is a chant that has an immediate effect when sung or repeated. I am often surprised that I find this chanted at spiritual gatherings. Its words mean Lord, have mercy.

Another beautiful religious chant is "Ti Ipermaho." This is a prayer to the Virgin Mary. There is a young boy by the name of Christos Santikai who chants "Ti Ipermaho." You can find it on YouTube. Even if you do not understand it, see if you feel a vibrational shift. https://www.youtube.com/watch?v=ysYIJ61LJgI\

If you have not used your religious practices in a while, you will find that bringing practices that have worked for you in your past will bring you more peace, faith, and connectedness.

Faith

"You can be anything you want to be, if only you believe with sufficient conviction and act in accordance with your faith; for whatever the mind can conceive and believe, the mind can achieve."
—Napoleon Hill

In Tony Robbins's *Unleash the Power Within* program, there is a fire walk where participants run across hot coals. During the fire walk, participants are repeating "Yes, yes," overriding every belief system that tells us that walking on hot coals will result in burned feet with the belief that "I can do this!"

The fire walk reminds me of a Bible story when Jesus was walking on water, and his disciple, Peter, asked if he could join him. As Peter was walking on water, he looked down at the water, realized that the water was turbulent, and started to sink. When he looked at Jesus, he was able to walk on the water. When he looked at the water, he started to sink.

Looking at our problems make them seem bigger than they actually are. This weakens us and makes us smaller than we actually are. Being preoccupied with problems make us sink. Faith pushes us up, allows us to run through coals unscathed, our faith allows us to know that we can do **anything**.

I remember the first time I went to a T. Harv Eker *Millionaire Mind* event. There was an exercise at the event, and all I will say is that it involved an arrow. The first time, I was one of the people who walked out during the arrow exercise. The last time I went I was given a plaque for having attended the program fifteen times. I had done the arrow exercise a total of fourteen times!

What changed? When I went the second time, I had the faith to know I was strong enough to not only do this exercise safely, but I knew I could do anything I put my mind to do. I would like to say that in both instances I was the same person, but I wasn't. When your mind changes, when fear is replaced by faith, you become a new version of yourself. You are no longer the same. Our potential is infinite.

Releasing Practices

Sometimes we accumulate so many things from our daily lives that we become stuck. For example, I love to cook, and on occasion when I am washing pots and pans, I find myself scrubbing a pot. If I have properly prepared the food, the scrubbing is minimal. But on occasion when something gets burned into the pot, it becomes a big job. I scrub and scrub for a long time to bring the pot to its original clean state. It is the same with our human self. We must make it a practice to release often. When in our life we accumulate anger, guilt, fear, just like a pot it takes a lot of scrubbing to find ourselves and think clearly.

For those with religious practices, you may release using traditional religious means. In my religion, several of the sacraments, including Holy Confession and Holy Communion, allow you to release and renew. I follow my religious practices in church weekly and throughout the year.

In my daily practices, I use some type of releasing process at a minimum twice a day. I use a combination of practices to release depending on the intensity of the situation. The Sedona Method is a releasing practice I use morning and night, to assure that my relationships are cleared.

Tapping is another popular method of release (EFT, Tapping Solution, Nick Ortner). This method has worked miracles for many of my friends and program participants. There is a "Tapping Solution" app by Nick and Jessica Ortner. Tapping physically reduces cortisol levels (fight or flight hormone) in your body and is a very effective way to release fears, anxiety, pain, physically and emotionally.

As mentioned before, Ho'oponopono is a lovely Hawaiian releasing practice (I use the song on YouTube).

When the situation is very difficult, or when a person has harmed me in some way, then the program that works best for me is *Vaporize Your Anxiety without Drugs or Therapy* by Tom Stone. The CORE technique described in it releases issues by seeing them as an energy form somewhere in our body. It is amazing to experience your emotion disappear as you zoom-focus on its core (center).

Tom Stone also presents an alternate method called the SEE technique. With this technique you access the edge of the energy of your emotion and go beyond it into the silence. Accessing the field of silence, you realize how small the emotional energy is compared to the infinite field of peace. As you explore the field of silence, which is infinite, you experience the shrinking of the emotional energy as your issue vaporizes. I would recommend that you use the methods that work best for you and support you best.

Ideas to Ponder

- We must remember that we have two jobs in life:

  - Love ourselves and one another.

  - Forgive ourselves and one another.

- Start the morning with a full dose of positivity:

  - Read something inspirational.

  - Remind yourself of all you are grateful for.

  - Pray.

  - Read your vision and affirmations (with emotion and enthusiasm).

  - Look at your day and release anything that you dread or look forward to.

  - Send Love and Light to those you love.

  - Send forgiveness to those who are causing struggle in your life.

- Ask for forgiveness from those you have hurt.

- Exercise and do an Energy routine.

- Midday Practices:

  - Ho'opono pono (I am sorry, please forgive me, I thank you, I love you)

  - Mantras meditation

  - Meditate (I enjoy the Big Mind Meditation)

- Night Practices

  - Vision and affirmations

  - Religious prayers

  - Releasing practice

- Important throughout-the-day practices:

  - The most important of all practices is Gratefulness. Approach your whole day with a grateful heart.

  - Approach your whole day with love in your heart, especially for those who enter your life experience.

  - Forgive everyone, but protect yourself from those who hurt you.

  - Walk away from abusive relationships. If you are in love with your abuser, treat it like an addiction. Protect yourself and love yourself.

- ○ Make raising your vibrational frequency a priority.

- If you have stepped away from your religious prayers, remember the ones that connected to your Spirit, and bring them back in your life.

- With faith we can move mountains and we can achieve anything we desire.

- Release negative emotions regularly.

Chapter 11

Waking Up

We know we are eternal, spiritual beings filled with love, yet we get to spend one hundred years or so on this earth. One hundred years in the context of eternity is maybe five minutes, or even less. We spend so much time of our life here on earth worrying about our problems. I often wonder what happens to all our problems when we die.

My mom used to be very obsessed about parking spaces in our street. Our home did not have a driveway or garage, and my mom wanted me to have a place to park when I came home from work late at night. Sometimes she would place a garbage can in a parking spot in order to hold it. Sometimes, if someone else parked in the parking spot in front of the house, she would ask them if they could park somewhere else because her daughter was almost home (that never worked, by the way).

Well, our neighbors had a huge issue with her. This had become the excuse to do bad things to us and be horrible to her. It was so bad that one day our neighbors across the street were talking to her, but she couldn't hear them. She started crossing the street in order to hear them better, and they called the police claiming she was going to attack them! Now there were four of them, and my mom was in her eighties and maybe 140 pounds.

It was a total surprise to me when every single one of these people came to her wake and funeral claiming to be her friends. Everything that had happened seemed to have evaporated upon her transition. I never brought up the past to them: I just moved on with my neighbors as my friends beyond her passing. So what happens to all our problems when we die? What happens to all the things we worry about? What happens to people who did bad things to us? Does everything just evaporate?

Experiencing our true self, we find that in reality there is only love, protection, abundance, health, joy. At any time, we can access this reality state of being. This is the state of being we read in the story of Adam and Eve prior to the fruit incident. The state where we are happy to give back to the world and be of service because we are filled with faith that all is well, and we are embraced with the light of God. Knowing our purpose puts us in a place of contribution that gives us clear direction on what we must do every day. Then we watch the wonder of synchronicity and miracles unfold in our lives.

Our human life is like a movie where we play several roles. Our roles may be a son, a daughter, a friend, a brother, a sister, a neighbor, a father, a mother, a colleague, and so many more. We play these roles the best we can as we contribute to each other's growth toward their next level of greatness. The other people in our life play their roles too.

Waking up is recognizing who we are and knowing that at any time we can access our true self. Our human self seems real and it feels real, and it is important because its goal is to make our soul rise to its next level of greatness. It is about feeling the joy of being on purpose. It is about coming full circle and knowing what we knew when we were babies.

Our goal every day is to express our love to everyone who enters our life. Through our meditation and prayer, it is knowing where we are supposed to be, finding those we are to support, and contributing to our purpose. My father seemed to know how to let go the small stuff and just bring joy to others. He always had his jokes and would do anything to spread happiness and make others laugh.

Waking up is realizing that we do not have to respond to everything that happens in our world. Waking up is realizing that all the little things that annoy us don't matter. And if an upset in your life is something big, you must know that you will be surrounded by people, angels, and God's light, and you will be filled with courage to do what you must do, knowing that you are not alone.

The only way to get out of terrible situations is by accessing your true self, envisioning your positive future, and doing what you must do at the right time. This could never include physically hurting anyone. I think of my amazing, lifelong friend, Marigo. She had to leave in the middle of the night to make sure that she and her babies were safe. It was a dangerous choice to get out, but she made it. It takes courage to do what you must do. It is so great seeing her now filled with happiness and laughter. When we talk about that night, she talks about her faith and about all the people and synchronicity of events that came together to help her through this.

Waking up is knowing that yesterday does not dictate your future. You can change your life immediately. Create your vision, repeat your affirmations, meditate, pray, know that the Universe is always working toward your good. Know that you are well and protected. Think of the last time you had a paper cut. Everything in your body rushed to heal it. The Universe is healing us constantly. We must wake up to see that physical, emotional, spiritual healing is taking place as long as we allow it. See the miracles in your life. Know that you can think of life as hard, or you can think of life as happy, joyous, abundant, loving. It is your life, and however you see it is how life will respond.

Waking up is realizing that everything in your life happened just as it should have. If everything in our life had not happened exactly as it did, you would not be who you are right now. Everything that happened in my life, all the struggles and pain, made me a stronger person; it made me who I am today.

When my ex-husband left, I thought it was the end of the world. I believed then that I could not go on. Now I know if he had not left, I would never have experienced all the great things I got to experience or met the amazing people that entered my life after he left. I would have most likely never have written this book. I now find myself so much happier and so much stronger than I was then.

He also seems to be a happier person. When I visited Greece in 2008, he invited me to lunch to meet his family. He was living in Greece with his new wife and twin children. They were all lovely. His wife was very nice, and his twins seemed so happy. He had found the family he wanted, he was in the country he wanted to live in, and I was so happy to see how perfectly everything had turned out. I was exactly where I wanted to be in life, and it was good to see him happy. My son was well and writing songs and writing and filming a movie at the time. It was a story that had turned out well for all.

Waking up means realizing that being human is like a dream and knowing that while we are alive we can still have access and choose to live in the light of God, feeling only love, knowing that we have everything we need, that we are always healing, and in our journey to feeling the joy, peace, security, and fulfillment that we crave. Spiritual and religious practices bring us to that true state. It is not allowing external events or other people derail our loving path. Understanding that no one can hurt our feelings or emotions without our permission. It takes letting go of fear and worry and replacing them with love and the faith that the Universe has given us all we need to experience our full potential.

Waking up is having faith that, like a caterpillar transforms into a butterfly, our transformation is a process and the next version of ourselves will be one step closer to the best version of ourselves. This life is filled with amazing experiences and miracles beyond our imagination. In order to experience them, we must be awake enough to see them and embrace them. We can let go and allow the perfect orchestration and synchronicity of the Universe to play out in our lives.

Miracles

When I was a teenager, my father developed a thyroid condition that affected his vision and made his eyes very swollen. He stayed at the Flower Hospital in New York for several weeks as they tried to diagnose what was making his eyes bulge and swell. The diagnosis was not good. They determined that it was caused by his thyroid. The loss of vision was due to the bulging and swelling and the effect on his optical nerves. The diagnosis confirmed that my father was going to be blind.

Wonderful people from the Association of the Blind came to visit our home to teach my father how to get around the house, how to shave, how to live as a blind man. My father's profession was a carpenter, so he couldn't work because it was such a huge risk having someone who can't see very well around the machinery. My father would lay on the couch, very depressed with his back to the TV.

One day he decided he was going to travel to Greece to see his brothers and sister and our family for the last time. It was August, and as he wanted to surprise everyone, he went to Greece unannounced. To his surprise, his relatives were not home! They had gone on vacation to the islands and different parts of Greece. The only relative that was home was one of my aunts from my mother's side, my aunt Ismini, who was very religious and lived alone.

As soon as my father arrived in her home, she told my father that they were going on another trip. She decided to take my father to the island of Tinos. This island is very popular to people in Greece but has not yet been discovered by tourists. The attraction is a church of the Virgin Mary that is known for its miracles. My aunt put my father in front of the icon of the Virgin Mary, told him to pray, and walked away. All he could see was shadows at this point, so my father had to stay where she left him because he was afraid he might get lost in the crowd and not be able to find her. He stood in front of the icon and began to pray. He could not see clearly, but he explained that he saw the shadow of a golden cross coming at him from the icon, and the energy pushed him back as it struck him in the forehead.

When he returned to the US from Greece, the condition of his eyes had worsened. His eye doctor was shocked as the eyes and nerves had been totally damaged, and according to the way things work, my father should have been blind. The unexplainable issue was that my father had almost perfect vision. He could now see perfectly! He continued driving and living his life normally. His doctor could not understand how my father could see at all! As a teenager I tried to explain to the doctor what had happened to my father in Greece, but the doctor totally dismissed it as an impossibility.

When I was growing up in Greece, I had visited the island of Tinos and this beautiful church. Back then, they gave tours and explained the miracles that had happened there that correlated to many gold items that had been donated to the church by families who had received the miracles. There was a lemon tree made of gold that was given to the church by the family of a girl that was born blind. When she was healed, the first thing she saw was the lemon tree outside of the church.

There was a golden vat donated to the church with a little hand coming up from the inside of the vat. It was explained that a little girl had fallen into a vat of hot oil. Her father was making *loukoumades* (Greek donuts) when his daughter fell in. The little girl fully recovered after visiting the church.

I grew up believing in miracles, as I had seen them at the island of Tinos, but my father's recovery was very personal. Between my father's healing and my personal visit to Tinos when I was young, I always expect miracles, and as a result have seen so many miracles in my life.

Albert Einstein said, "Do you believe in miracles? Well, you should. In fact, life itself is a big miracle. There are so many things that are beyond our understanding. There are two ways to live: You can live as if nothing is a miracle; you can live as if everything is a miracle."

The thing about miracles is that in order to know they are happening, you must expect them and look for them. There are so many miracles I see in my life, and also in other people's lives. Often I have to bring them to their attention. People miss how amazing they are, what they bring to the world, and all the extraordinary things that happen at just the right moment in order to bring things on course. Know how amazing you are, all that you bring to the world, and notice the amazing miracles around you.

Synchronicity

Several years ago, I was a parish council member at my church. I was asked to interview a priest, Father Demetrios Constantelos. He was a priest at my church in the 1960s. He was coming back to visit the church at the invitation of the Parish Council President, fifty years later. The visit was going to be videotaped, and I was going to conduct the interview. What was incredible about Father Constantelos is, when he joined our church in the 1950s, it had about 150 families. When he left to pursue other endeavors, the church had over 400 families.

As the church had some major renovations done, we thought that the visit would be fulfilling for him to see that his old parish was still doing well, even though the membership had dropped again. During the interview, it was quickly apparent that I was speaking to someone holy, with extraordinarily deep wisdom and grace. You could see in his eyes his love for the church, for the people, and for God. It was a surprise that he seemed to remember people from all those years ago, and he was asking if everyone was well, as though he had been with them recently.

He shared with me insights that highlighted how every single day was driven by his purpose and perfect orchestration by God. His being, his compassion, is what had attracted people to the church. He indicated that he always noticed who was in the church services and who was not. If someone didn't come to service, he would call them to see if everything was all right. People who didn't come to church knew that they would hear from the priest that week, and, as a result, came to church regularly. They had found someone who cared for their well-being and spiritual growth.

I asked him why he left our church since the congregation was so happy and growing, and everything was so successful. He told me how important it is that in our daily prayers we ask God to place us where we can be of service. He indicated he did this every day and just followed God's lead. That's why he had to leave. He was needed for God's next assignment. He told me to always know that God not only listens but also answers us. All we have to do is listen for His answer.

After leaving our church community, he found himself teaching at Princeton University, writing many books, and traveling around the world giving lectures and changing lives. He had spent a lifetime following God's direction, and that brought him peace and joy. He opened his life to God and just followed the flow. Father Constantelos passed away shortly after that interview.

My life has changed since that day. When you follow his advice and follow God's lead, you will find your whole life in total synchronicity. I used to worry about the timing of things; now I know that the timing is always perfect. Going through open doors, without knowing why, knowing that what is about to happen is orchestrated, provides me with confidence, peace, and joy. I trust that everything is perfectly synchronized and expect serendipity. My friend Linda calls them coincidences. It is fine. How many coincidences could there be in a given day? In mine there are hundreds, but I am aware of them.

In the past I would not even notice them, but now everything seems connected and things always fall into place. This is where time plays tricks on us. Out of character things that I did years ago or months ago seem to fall into place with a perfect purpose now. Everything is in perfect, what I call, "synchrony." And out of character things that I do today, I know will become of purpose at some point in the future.

The Library

A few years ago during meditation, I kept hearing the word "library." As I work from home, I didn't immediately react because I didn't know what it meant. One day I sat at the end of my street trying to make a decision when, of course, I thought I was late going into the office. Do I turn left to go to work, or do I make a right to go to the library? My logical mind was telling me to make a left, but I made a right. I walked into the library and stood there, not knowing what I was supposed to do next.

"Can I help you?" said the librarian.

"I don't know," I answered.

She asked, "Do you have a library card?"

I answered, "No."

She said, "Why don't we get you one while you are deciding."

She took out a form and asked me to fill it out. As I returned it, she asked if I had any time to volunteer at the library.

I immediately answered, "No." At that time, I was working full time, teaching a popular professional development course at night, and coaching several clients. I couldn't imagine finding the time to do anything else.

On the top of the counter was Jack Canfield's book *Success Principles.* Only one month before, my friends and I had purchased a row of seats at Jack Canfield's event. At the back of the event workbook, Jack had invited participants to present the course to others, and since it was part of giving back to the world, we were not to charge for it. He also provided us with slides and the student workbook in case we had the opportunity to share.

"Have you heard of Jack Canfield?" the librarian asked.

"Yes, I got to see him a month ago! I think I have the slides and could definitely present the materials to anyone who is interested in our city."

She was so happy to offer this course on behalf of the library. The group of people this class attracted was amazing. It seemed to be the perfect course, with everyone bonding, transforming, and sharing. We expanded the course to run more weeks than anticipated as the participants did not want it to end. At the end of this experience, I understood what the word "library" had meant, and I was so glad I listened to my heart rather than my brain the day I thought I was late for work.

The library experience felt like it was orchestrated and perfectly synchronized in my life. There was no doubt in my mind that the course I taught there was exactly what was supposed to happen. The word "library" that I heard during meditation, the librarian talking about Jack Canfield's book, the people that showed up at the class is a perfect example of synchronicity. That's when I realized that perhaps my whole life has been a series of perfectly orchestrated events.

The Impossible Becomes Possible

Someone like me was not supposed to go to college. We had come to the United States for the first time when I was in sixth grade. For seventh grade, we were back in Greece. In the middle of eighth grade, we were back in the US. My parents both worked at factories--my father making kitchen cabinets, my mother making leather jackets. They were both making close to minimum wage. Yet there was no doubt in my mind that I was going to go to college. I was in the college preparatory program in high school, with my guidance counselors strongly recommending that I choose a different path since it was so obvious college was not going to be in my future. To keep everyone satisfied, I took a typing class and a steno class while still in the college prep program.

A nearby chemical company came to the school and asked for a girl from high school to join them in the work-school program. My teacher did not have enough junior girls in the secretarial program to send for the interview, so she sent me, assuring me I was not going to get the job. When I went on the interview, I shared that I was going to college (even though I had no idea how this was going to happen), and assuring them that I would not be a good candidate to select since I was not interested in being a secretary. I was going to leave them after senior year to go to college. Despite all this, I was hired. I had applied to Rutgers, struggling to come up with the money to pay for the application.

Somehow, due to a question in my records, I visited the campus, and I got to talk to the dean, Richard McCormick. I told him that although I wanted to go to Rutgers, even if I was admitted, I most likely would not be able to attend. I explained we had recently come from Greece, and my parents didn't have the resources to send me to college. He asked if I knew how to type. I told him I had been working for a chemical company as a secretary for over a year.

I got to work in Dean McCormick's office full time, while going to school full time. I had two majors, International Business and Political Science. My tuition was paid by the University since I was a full-time employee. In my junior year, AT&T International was opening, and I was recruited. They paid for my senior year tuition, and my career started.

Through a series of happenstances, everything fell into place. My vision to graduate from Rutgers became a reality. Taking a typing and steno class got me the job at the chemical company, which was a stepping-stone to getting my free tuition at Rutgers by working full time in the dean's office. I got to work for AT&T International doing exactly what I studied.

At the chemical company, I got to work with the mayor of a nearby city. He was so proud of his city and always told me I should move there. When my parents decided to buy a house, well, we ended up moving to this city, where I have lived now for forty-five years. Everything was a perfect orchestration of events. If all my expectations were based on human expectations, given all the limitations in my life at that time, I would have never applied to a college. My life would have been totally different and very much compromised.

When you let go and have the faith, knowing that the Universe will move mountains in order for you to experience your greatness, your life will change. Never look at your current circumstances to determine what you will reach in life. What you will reach in life is based on your purpose, your visions, and the contributions that you make in the evolution of the Universe. Yes, you are that important! You have a major role to play in the trajectory of the future of the world. We read history and are often amazed as how much certain individuals changed history, yet the whole time, we also are living lives that will impact the world. All you need to do is become aligned with it all.

Friends

A good way to see the synchronicity in your life is to reflect on how you met your friends. You will find that these special people appeared in your life and how without them you would have never been able to achieve amazing things, or even handle some of the difficult things in your life.

My dear friend, Marigo, kept saying, "Hi, Maria" to me at college as we passed each other on campus in between classes. I didn't know who she was or how she knew my name. One day as she walked by and said, "Hi Maria," I stopped and asked her how she knew me because I didn't know who she was. She looked at me closer and told me I reminded her of her friend, Maria. I told her my name was Maria too. We laughed and instantly connected.

One day walking on campus, I saw this beautiful young woman who did not look like me, but I knew it had to be Marigo's friend, Maria! Maria and I looked at each other and started laughing as we both said at the same time, "Maria?" The three of us were inseparable throughout our college years. Although Maria's career brought her to Greece, the three of us, Maria, Marigo, and me (Maria), have been so very close to this day. These ladies are my forever friends, and when tracing back how we met, it was miraculous.

I met my friend Wendy at the Division of Motor Vehicles while getting my driver's license renewed. I had waited until the very last day because at that time my mother had Alzheimer's disease, and I couldn't leave her alone at home in order to get my license. Not knowing what to do, on the last day before my license expired, I took my mom with me to the DMV and asked her to sit in the car for a few minutes.

I was filling out forms and running out to the car to check on my mother to make sure she was okay. As I was walking out with my renewed license, this beautiful lady reached out to talk to me. I told her I had to run, as my mother was in the car. She ended up being a true angel in my life. We exchanged phone numbers, and Wendy actually called me several times, always asking how I was doing, and how my mother was doing.

When my mother passed away, and a few weeks later I lost my job, and a few weeks later my engagement ended,

Wendy was there for me with compassion and love. We were both at the DMV at the same time. I was in a hurry, and she is by nature a shy person. What are the chances that we would meet, and even talk on that day? Yet we were supposed to know each other. Wendy has been there for me through so many hurdles in my life. I feel so blessed having Wendy in my life as my forever friend.

My friend Anna Marie was the smiling face at the office. She was the person at the front desk, always positive and supportive to everyone who worked at my company. When she left the company, she was missed by everyone, but especially me. I called her to tell her how much I missed her, and we started meeting for coffee. Anna Marie and her husband, Tom, will always be my so very special friends in my life.

When I was told I needed hip surgery, I didn't think I had the strength and courage to do it. Anna Marie and Tom were right there with me through the whole process. They even brought me to the hospital and were always there for me. The hospital was three hours away from their home. They not only brought me to the hospital, they brought me home, and they even came to see me while I was in the hospital. You could never adequately express gratefulness to God for special friends like these, nor could you ever express adequate appreciation to special people like this.

When I started working at AT&T, I met Mike, who seemed to know everyone in the company. Mike was from Cyprus and seemed to especially know people who were of Greek descent. Throughout the years Mike has remained a genuine, great friend. I had met his wife, Stacy, several times at different Greek and church events. When I lost my job, Stacy called me to see how I was, and she asked me to send her my resume. After receiving it, she re-engineered it and made it professional and perfect. Stacy is my angel on earth! She is always there through good times and bad times, a woman of great faith, compassion, and so much love in her heart. She is another special friend that I am so very grateful for.

My friend Linda and I sat across from each other at our then Toastmasters Club. Several times throughout the meetings, we would look at each other and just laugh. Both Linda and I stopped being members of that particular Toastmasters Club, but for the last fourteen years we talk for hours every weekend. I can't imagine a weekend without talking to Linda. She is another true blessing in my life.

And then it is the synchronicity of a very special family in my life. When I first started working at AT&T, I shared an office with the most incredible young lady, who I called Lucy. We became inseparable during the years of dating, getting married, being married, well, until my divorce.

As I was entering the single life again, another best friendship from work emerged. It was my friend, Margi. Margi was one of my closest friends for twenty years. Well, Margi is Lucy's sister. Then work got in the way. She was in a job where she traveled a lot, and we lost touch.

As I started spending time at my customers' locations, I became friends with some amazing people. As I had a tendency to work late at night, I became good friends with someone who also worked late. We would spend time catching up, and every time we talked, it felt like he was family. He was Margi's and Lucy's brother. This family has always felt like my family. And as time goes on, I get to know in-depth all its members.

When my son was a baby, their mother, Mrs. J., who was a nurse, had the magic touch. Any time my son was fussy I would put him in the car to visit my friends. The minute Mrs. J. touched Georgio, he would stop fussing and fall asleep. There is such a divine closeness with this family, a true blessing.

I can write another book just talking about how I met all my very special friends. Ken, Robert, Rafael, Lori who were by my side when teaching self-development programs and workshops years ago, and are still in my life as such very special friends. I can write a book about the beautiful children that came into my life for me to teach, yet they have taught me the most important lessons.

Through the years, they grew up to be amazing people, and I am so grateful to have some as my lifelong friends, and others appear again, and I know they are all okay. The list is just too long! Every single person showed up when I needed them, or I showed up when they needed me. They are friends I am blessed with and I treasure. Every single person is a true miracle in my life.

Letting Go of Worry

As humans, we can't help but worry, but it is useless. We will find that whatever we worry about will most likely never happen. On the other hand, things we don't expect may appear. The

Coronavirus pandemic is an example. Everyone had worries in their life, but it is doubtful that anyone worried about a pandemic that would make so many people sick and would take so many lives.

It was only a few years ago that I did worry sometimes. I would need to remind myself that I had allowed myself to get tangled up in the fear of unlikely possibilities. I had to replace fear with faith, replace worry with love. It is then wise to embrace our vision rather than worry about the status quo.

We don't know what the future holds, but we do know that if we anticipate great experiences in our future, there is a good possibility that this is what we will attract. We know when we are grateful, when we have faith, when we are filled with positive energy, all worry goes away. When something feels like it's bigger than us, we remind ourselves that it is time to grow spiritually. When we grow bigger than our problems, our problems seem very small and manageable. Using the practices in this book moves our life toward positive growth and experiencing the joy of living an intentional, purposeful life.

And then something magical happens. It is the realization that everything in your life has been perfectly synchronized and is continuously moving you toward your good. This is the moment when all your worries go away. This is also the moment when you realize that everything and everyone in your life has an important purpose. In the last several years it feels like my life is flowing and all I have to do is let go and be transported to the next great experience. Where in the past it felt like I was on a fast train to nowhere, full of stress and worry, where everything moved so fast I couldn't even see the view, while the stress and worry devoured my life experience. Now it feels like I am fully feeling and experiencing life. As people enter my life I acknowledge that I am there for a purpose, and that they are there for a purpose. I embrace them with love, and watch as things unfold.

Even sitting in a traffic jam feels like it has a purpose, and I embrace it knowing that things are unfolding as they should. The weird thing is that since I started experiencing life in this mode, regardless of what happens, I seem to always arrive in perfect timing, not a minute before or after I should have arrived. When you begin noticing everything in your life is when you will see that everything and everyone is a miracle.

And this is when I realized that even when we think we have reached our level of greatness, there is always a next level of our greatness that follows. As we start thinking we have to control everything, we find ourselves realizing that everything is already under perfect control. If we allow ourselves to get into this flow, we realize there is nothing to worry about. There is an expectation that everything in the past, in the present, and in the future is just as it should be.

The Caterpillar

A long time ago I saw a picture of a mountain made up of caterpillars that were trying to get to the top, trying to reach their greatness. We sometimes say that some people try to get to the top by stepping on others in order to get there. This picture showed caterpillars piled up as they stepped on each other to get to the top. There were a few caterpillars that had reached the top because they had stepped on caterpillars below them. You could see the bottom layer of caterpillars was getting crushed, yet more caterpillars were joining the journey to the top, stepping on each other and injuring each other in the process. Off to the side were some caterpillars that just refused to step on others. They also wanted to reach the top, but not by injuring others. They had a better way.

In human terms, we normally view the ones who step aside and choose to not hurt anyone in order to get ahead as the ones who will lose. In human terms there are winners and losers and by not participating, it means you will lose the race. The picture showed a different story. In reality, it is not a competition at all. We are all one. It was interesting to see in the picture what happened to the caterpillars on the sidelines. You see, the caterpillars that stepped aside transformed into beautiful butterflies, and they reached the top that way. Perhaps all caterpillars know their potential to become a butterfly, and this may make it easier to step aside. We are not very different. I had seen this picture early on in my career, and it made it so much easier to know the right choices in business and in life.

Waking up is knowing who we are and letting go of fear. It is knowing that inside you there is the potential of boundless beauty, freedom, and ability to reach heights beyond our imagination. Waking up is knowing and choosing to reach our potential by letting go. It is knowing that our potential is beyond what our eyes can see. Even though a caterpillar may not know that it will develop beautiful wings and have the ability to fly, the ones that step aside have the faith to know that a transformation will occur and something beautiful beyond imagination will emerge. We all know that something beyond our human capacity and understanding is at work. We must allow our greatness to emerge so we can reach our full potential. The purpose of our life is to experience pure joy as we become the very best version of ourselves in fulfilling our life purpose.

Ideas to Ponder

- Waking up is the moment we enter a world of deep wisdom, awareness, and consciousness. Spontaneously we are fully embraced in a world where we are all connected and one, everything is love, abundance, eternal, peaceful, joyful, and everything runs through divine orchestration and synchronicity.

- Waking up is discovering our true self and being able to live life from a state of total connection with God.

- Our life becomes one of life purpose and contribution toward this purpose.

- Waking up is entering a world of miracles, where things happen beyond our human understanding and limitations.

- Waking up is experiencing life fully and embracing the expansion of our soul toward the next level of our greatness.

- Everyone who enters our life is a miracle; we are meant to approach each other with kindness and love.

- Waking up is realizing that the small things that upset us are not important. It is the realization that we are meant to remain who we are regardless of what is happening around us. Responding to insults, jealousy, takes us out of our rhythm and into the world of human pain.

- When large upsets are in your life, being awake is knowing that people, angels, and God's light is surrounding you and healing you as you are going through your difficult situation.

- Everything that happened in your past brought you to this moment.

- Every new version of yourself can be one step closer to the best version of you.

- Be awake in order to notice the miracles, synchronicity, serendipity in your life.

- We must trust in the perfect orchestration and synchronicity of the Universe.

- You don't have to struggle to get to the top. There is a transformation (butterfly) inside of you.

- The impossible becomes possible in order for you to reach your purpose and destiny.

- If you carefully look at how you met your friends, you will notice the serendipity of the Universe.

- Changing fear to faith, seeing all as one, coming from a place of love and your true self, makes your worry to evaporate.

- When we see how the Universe is embracing us with people, angels, experiences that enter our lives, we realize that the Universe is moving us toward healing and betterment. And when we realize that everything is in perfect synchronicity and orchestration, then we know there is nothing to worry about.

- Worrying holds onto status quo. Faith, vision, affirmations, moves us forward toward our life purpose.

- Know who you are. You are a spiritual being having a human experience with purpose and the ability to continuously move toward your next level of transformation.

Chapter 12

Conclusion: Greatness

Minimizing the Blow of Future Breakdowns

Throughout the years I have been privileged to teach personal/professional development courses, fulfilling my life purpose. Becoming a Certified Trainer for Jack Canfield's Success Principles Program allowed me to touch even more people's lives. When we open our mind, allow a shift in our thinking, when we let go and allow Universal flow, a transformation happens. As participants' lives transformed, I found myself uplifted to a new level. There are so many people in my programs who believe they are the only ones experiencing a certain tsunami in their life. Every time they find several other people in the program going through the same experience or having gone through the same experience. How they come out of it seems to be a matter of perspective.

And how we come out of our tsunami depends on how we approach it; it's a matter of perspective. A tsunami can kill us, or it can lift us to our next level of greatness. The result depends on our perspective, our reaction, our approach, and our understanding of the possibility of perfection of what just happened.

So how do we minimize the blow of future breakdowns? By knowing that breakdowns are part of our life journey and having the wisdom to know that they lead us to our current greatness. Know that no event ever determines your final outcome. It is only your response that determines the level of trauma or joy you experience and determines the trajectory of what will happen in your future.

It may not be trauma at all. If the purpose of life is reaching our highest spiritual potential, the very best version of ourselves, then breakdowns are an accelerated elevation toward that potential. The person that you are today is a different person than who you will be one year from now and especially five years from now. Problems that you are facing now will not even affect you next time. You will be wiser and greater.

The secret is knowing and relaxing, understanding that everything in the Universe is a perfect synchrony. When we fill ourselves with the love that we are, we can sit back and go with the flow of pure joy. We may not know if it was serendipity, synchronicity, happenstance, or a miracle, but when great things happen, do we really care?

Experiencing Your Levels of Greatness

The movie *The Switch* starts with the following quote. "Look at us. Running around, always rushed, always late. I guess that's why they call it the human race. What we crave most in this world is connection."

At the end of the movie, the quote is stated again, but a bit differently. "Every once in a while, out of all the randomness, something unexpected happens that pushes us all forward. And the truth is, what I'm struggling to think, and what I'm struggling to feel, is that maybe the human race isn't a race at all."

In my teens, I had no idea how, but I knew I was going to college. When I was in college, I didn't know how, but I just knew I was going to be working for a big company in my field. When I got to the big company all I could see was the "human race." It was a competitive environment where I was a woman in a man's world. I didn't know how, but I became the level I wanted to become in the big company.

As I taught a top professional development course, I realized that there is only one type of competition, and that is with yourself. It is the competition of knowing that every day you bring to the table a new version of yourself. One that is a greater version as it has within it the lessons and wisdom of the day before.

It is a great revelation when we realize that we are all one. We all feel the pain of our human-ness, we feel our pain and each other's pain as we are all connected. It is a great revelation to know that hurting anyone is hurting everyone and hurting ourselves. With every revelation, with every tsunami in my life, with every new version of myself I thought this was it! This was my greatness! I had achieved a wisdom that had elevated me to a new level. This had to be it! Especially when I realized that we have the ability to transform and change our experience.

It was fun to learn about the Law of Attraction. Knowing this is how the Universe works, and I could attract through my vision and affirmations the things I wanted in my life made me think I was again in control. This was my greatness. I suddenly realized that the Law of Attraction is an important step, but it is only a step, it is not the arrival. How many more steps are there? I suspect unlimited. But that doesn't mean that every level of greatness does not deserve a pause, a reflection of the wisdom gained, a celebration of wisdom and life.

For me, letting go and embracing the sanctity of the Universal flow is my current level of greatness. The voice I hear tells me that my life purpose is just part of a melody. The things I love, the things in my visions and affirmations are already part of that symphony. And as though a curtain has been opened, I see that everything flows in its rhythm and time.

I hope this book unblocks your way and you embrace this beautiful journey called our life. Wherever you are in your journey, consider "Greatness" a graduation to your next level of wisdom, understanding, and next version of yourself. I know there are beautiful things ahead for you.

The human race is not a race at all. It is a joyful, spiritual journey to your next level of greatness. In your journey you will come to some crossroads. You will have to make a choice between your human self or your true self, the clay or the gold, between fear or faith, between ego or love, between upward movement or stillness. Go for the gold, choose faith, live from the love within, always move upward, accept the abundance, and follow the flow of being of service to those who enter your experience. It is definitely a journey, even though so many live their lives as though it is a destination.

Enjoy the journey to Your Greatness!!

Ideas to Ponder

- Whatever issue you are facing, although you may feel alone, you are not alone. Although it feels like you are the only one who is going through something like this, it is not true.

- Tsunamis can kill you or lift you to the next level of greatness. Be lifted.

- Our reaction to tsunamis determines the outcome.

- The more tsunamis we go through, the easier it becomes to overcome them.

- Tsunamis are an accelerated promotion toward our next level of greatness.

- Purpose of life is to become the best version of ourselves and to reach our highest potential.

- As we become wiser and greater, old problems become smaller and are minimized.

- Life is a series of stepping stones of wisdom and learnings. We reach milestones that become our greatness.

- Finding our true self and readily accessing it is one of these milestones of greatness. Understanding the Universal Laws and the Law of Attraction is yet another milestone of greatness. Understanding synchronicity, serendipity, miracles, is yet another level. And there are many more.

- The levels of greatness are unlimited; the goal is to reach as many levels as possible.

To your Greatness!

Acknowledgements

With an open heart, I followed the synchronicity and flow of the Universe that brought me to Christine. Without Christine and her team, this book would have taken many years to write, and I am not sure if it would have ever made it out into the world. Thank you so much Christine, Jean, and Carrie!!

I would like to thank my brilliant son, Georgio. Thank you, Georgio, for your love and support. You are truly the best son a mother could ever wish for. Without your encouragement, it would not have been possible to write this book.

Thank you to my family in the United States. My aunt Niki for always reminding me that I am a "prigipessa" (princess) and I can accomplish anything. I would like to thank my cousin Peter and beautiful Leslie; you have both always been there for me. You are in my heart, and I always feel your love and support. Thank you to my beautiful cousin Elena. You have kept me afloat during rough tsunamis in my life, and I love you so much. I am grateful to my other cousin Peter; we got to know each other as children, and played in the summer at our grandmother's house. I got to see your kindness and sweetness as a child. It is so great to see you successful now in all you do.

I am so grateful to my uncle Pete and my aunt Elsie, without whom I would have had a different life. They made it possible for me and my parents to come to the United States, the land of so many opportunities and possibilities. We stayed in their home, and my cousins Peter, Michael, and Elena became the brothers and baby sister I never had as an only child. We spent almost two years of joy living in the same home as one family. I am so grateful for this wonderful time and the deep love that continually gets stronger as we grow older and cherish the memories.

Thank you to my family in Greece, who always checked up on me and encouraged me to continue to work on this book. Thank you Ada, Kiki, Marino, Marina, Vasili, Grigori, Maria, Yianni, Elaine, Voula, Eleni, Dimitra, Thea Evgenia, Peter, Eleni, Vaso, Xanthi, and Dimitra. I love you all so much.

Thank you so much, Wendy and Linda, for being such amazing friends and the first to read the book. Your ideas, feedback, notes, and often redirection were treasures. Thank you for your time and dedication; this was a lot of work, and every minute you spent supporting me and the writing of this book is so greatly appreciated.

Thank you to my friends Anna Marie, Tom, Ken, Robert, Lori, Angie, Rafael, Ann, Melissa for sticking with me, even though I was no longer available on weekends and evenings, and for all your encouragement. I always feel blessed when I am with you and treasure every minute we get to experience life together.

Thank you to my friends Marigo and Maria. We found each other in college and got to share our life together as lifelong friends. You are the true example that we are all connected through our hearts, and physical distance just doesn't matter.

I would like to thank the people that God brought into my life to teach. Actually, you are all my teachers. I love you Debbie, Olga, Nikie, Stacey, Effie, Spiro, Mike, Eva, Lenna, Joanne, and to all my "kids." You are so very precious to me; regardless of how old we all become, you will always be my kids.

Thank you to my work family. You have always checked up on me and encouraged me to continue writing this book. Michael K., Christian D., you have encouraged me to write this book even when it was a series of ideas written down informally over ten years ago. Thank you to my current wonderful work family: Achim, Annette, Thomas W., Christian, Michael, Federico, Martin, and Thomas K. in Germany; Wagner, Rogerio, Roberto, Andre, William, Estevam, Deborah in Brazil; Alan in Singapore; Chris and Tina in UK; George in China; and Adam, Eszter, and Balint in Hungary. Special appreciation to my friends and work colleagues in the US: Regis, Eric, Shawna, Russ, Nick, Francis, George, Dave, Andy, Janice, Jimmy, Jay, Oscar. We got to experience several tsunamis together. It has been such a privilege sharing our professional and personal growth together from so many experiences. I am so very grateful for the serendipity and synchronicity that brought us all together.

References

In this space I will acknowledge some of the programs that have transformed my life and practices that have become part of who I am.

Dale Carnegie Programs

Jack Canfield, *Success Principles*

Tony Robbins Programs

T. Harv Eker, *The Secrets of the Millionaire Mind*

Stephen Covey, *The 7 Habits of Highly Effective People*

Genpo Roshi, *Big Mind, Big Heart: Finding Your Way*

Oprah Winfrey, *Live Your Best Life*

Christine Kloser, *The Freedom Formula*

Byron Katie, *The Work*

Tom Stone, *Vaporize your Anxiety*

Hale Dwoskin, *The Sedona Method*

Nick Ortner, *The Tapping Solution*

Donna Eden, *Eden Energy Medicine*

Louise Hay, *You Can Heal Your Life*

Don Miguel Ruiz, *The Four Agreements*

Wayne Dyer, *The Power of Intention*

Eckhart Tolle, *The New Earth*

Marci Shimanoff, *Happy for No Reason* and Year of Miracles Program

Sue Morter, *Energy Codes*

About the Author

Maria Mantoudakis is an author, award-winning motivational speaker, professional transformational leader, and personal development coach. In May 2008, Maria was ranked as one of the top two speakers in New York and New Jersey by Toastmasters International.

In addition, Maria Mantoudakis is Client Lead at British Telecom Americas. Her work experience includes a more than a thirty-year career with British Telecom, AT&T, Lucent Technologies, and Alcatel. She has also recently launched her company for personal development and transformation, **ReCreate Success Now**.

Maria's passion is in the areas of personal and professional development, that includes motivational speaking, coaching, leadership, and transformation. She is a former Certified Instructor of the **Dale Carnegie Course**™ which she taught for fifteen years. In December 2008, Maria was honored by being in the top ten-percentile ranking of instructors around the world.

In January 2017, Maria became a Certified Trainer of the **Jack Canfield Success Principles Program**. The Jack Canfield **Success Principles Program** focuses on intentional living through the creation and realization of life purpose and success utilizing Universal principles

Maria offers personal development and life coaching programs through her newly formed company, **ReCreate Success Now**. Her programs challenge individual comfort zones resulting in professional and personal development, leadership, achievement of life purpose, and transformational goals.

CONNECT WITH THE AUTHOR:
Website: RecreateSuccessNow.com
Or you may write Maria: recreatesuccessnow@gmail.com
Linktree: linktr.ee/mantoudakis